The Complete Guide to

Surviving Contracts
for Voluntary Organisations

**Alan Lawrie
Jan Mellor**

DIRECTORY OF SOCIAL CHANGE

Published by
Directory of Social Change
24 Stephenson Way
London NW1 2DP
Tel. 08450 77 77 07; Fax 020 7391 4804
E-mail publications@dsc.org.uk
www.dsc.org.uk
from whom further copies and a full books catalogue are available.

Directory of Social Change is a Registered Charity no. 800517

First published 2008

Copyright © Directory of Social Change 2008

The moral right of the author has been asserted in accordance with the Copyright, Designs and Patents Act 1988.

All rights reserved. **No part of this book may be stored in a retrieval system or reproduced in any form whatsoever without prior permission in writing from the publisher.**
This book is sold subject to the condition that it shall not, by way of trade or otherwise, be lent, re-sold, hired out or otherwise circulated without the publisher's prior permission in any form of binding or cover other than that in which it is published, and without a similar condition including this condition being imposed on the subsequent purchaser.

ISBN 978 1 903991 94 7

British Library Cataloguing in Publication Data

A catalogue record for this book is available from the British Library

Cover and text designed by Stephen Strong
Typeset by Stephen Strong
Printed and bound by Page Bros

All Directory of Social Change departments in London:
08450 77 77 07

Directory of Social Change Northern Office:
Research 0151 708 0136

Contents

Foreword iv

Introduction v

1. Approaching contracts 1
The themes of this book 1
Features of traditional grant-aid relationships 1
Features of contractual relationships 2
What is driving the move to contracts? 3
The five prerequisites of successful contract management 4
Thriving in the contract culture 5
Funding mechanisms 6
What sort of relationships are possible? 7

2. All about contracts 9
Contracts today 9
Commissioning principles for public service organisations 10
The language of a contract 12
The different types of contract 15

3. The process of contracting 17
Legal background 17
Best value and 'the four Cs' 18
Engaging with the commissioning process 19
The choice of procurement procedure 21
Getting onto the tender list 22
The invitation to tender 22
Evaluation of the tender 23
What happens if things go wrong? 24

4. Analysing an opportunity 27
Responding to a contract opportunity 27
What is in a specification? 27
Evaluating a specification 28
Analysing a specification 30
Identifying the risks involved in taking on a service 32
The relevance of the specification 33
Making the decision to bid 34

5. Making a bid 35
Elements of a successful bid 35
Analysing and understanding the bidding process 35
Identifying what your organisation can offer 37
Costing and pricing your bid 39
Writing the bid document 45
Bid presentations and interviews 47
Your bid checklist 51

6. Agreeing a contract 53
Model agreements 54
Avoiding common problems 54
Termination of the contract 55
Legal issues related to tendering 56
Before entering a contract consider… 56
Negotiating the agreement 57

7. Managing the contract 69
Types of contract relationship 69
Factors influencing the relationship 70
Measuring the performance of the contract 71
Measuring outcomes 72
Designing and agreeing performance measures 73
Dealing with problems and changes 74
Designing processes to deal with problems 75
Building a relationship with the commissioner 76
Managing the end of the contract 77

8. The organisational implications of contracts 79
The importance of organisational culture 79
Organisational sustainability 80
Protecting and managing independence 84
The role of the board of trustees 85
Organisational capacity 86
Business planning issues 87

9. Competition, cooperation and future possibilities 89
Operating in a market atmosphere 89
How to analyse your market 90
The issue of competition 91
Working together 92
Working together in a contract environment 92
Looking ahead to future trends 97

Further reading and resources 99

Index 101

Foreword

For any charity, it is likely that at some point you will be offered the chance to undertake an activity which will be funded through a contractual arrangement. Indeed, over the last decade, that likelihood has increased significantly as the nature of statutory funding has both increased and become more dependent on conditions.

For the charity, its staff and trustees, the prospect of contract income can be extremely attractive. It may offer the opportunity to deliver that project, or employ that member of staff that really allows you to achieve your goals. It may be the stepping stone to a larger, more influential organisation. On the face of it, writing a tender for funds with four, five, six or even (rarely) seven figures, looks a hell of a lot easier than a tin rattle outside Tesco in the rain in November raising £25.40.

However, the possibilities do have their down sides. The risks are numerous – have you got the funding balance right? Have you built in sufficient overhead costs? Have you undersold yourself? Have you oversold yourself?

Perhaps the biggest question is – have you considered the impact upon your organisation? I know of organisations that started with just a couple of contracts, then it mushroomed, and suddenly it's 85 per cent of their income. Is that what you want to do as a charity? Might this threaten your independence? In the drive for more money, do you run the risk of losing sight of your values? Oh, and when was the last time, you tin-rattled in Tesco?

That's why this book is so timely. I know from working with Mind's 180 local associations, that the realities of contracting are both exciting and frightening, opportunities and risks. As the recently published NCVO *UK Voluntary Sector Almanac* showed, it's the only area where income generating is growing for the voluntary sector, and it looks like it's here to stay. In my personal experience, the organisations I've worked for have managed to be clear that they may well receive contract income, but it doesn't compromise their campaigning work.

You can't ignore it, but if you decide to play the game, you have to go into it knowing the rules and with your eyes wide open. So read on and enjoy!

Paul Farmer
Chief Executive
Mind

Introduction

This book aims to help managers and trustees of voluntary organisations navigate their way through the various decisions, concepts and implications of bidding for and negotiating contracts and agreements with public sector organisations.

It is mainly based on interviews with managers who have successfully (and in some cases unsuccessfully) been involved in contracting, and with commissioning staff in local authorities, the NHS and other organisations. While researching the book we came across a lot of confusion, anxiety and over-involvement in detail, all of which obscured managers' engagement in the bigger picture. At the heart of the book therefore is the message that if voluntary organisations choose to bid for contracts they must do so in a way that protects and develops their independence and ensures the longer-term sustainability of the organisation. No voluntary organisation wishes to end up as little more than a subservient and low cost sub-contractor of the public sector. We hope that this book will play some part in helping your organisation avoid such a scenario.

We are grateful to all the individuals who gave up their time to share their experiences, and to our various consultancy clients and participants in training programmes who have helped us to shape our ideas.

We would particularly like to thank Lynne Laidlaw, London VCS Project Manager at Clinks, for commenting on an early draft and Lawrence Simanowitz and Mairead O'Reilly, partner and solicitor respectively, at Bates Wells & Braithwaite for their comments and advice.

Jan Mellor
Alan Lawrie
October 2007

Jan Mellor and Alan Lawrie are independent management consultants specialising in management and organisational development.

Approaching contracts

The idea of voluntary organisations bidding for and negotiating contracts with statutory bodies has generated a considerable amount of debate, controversy and anxiety. It has raised questions about the different roles of statutory bodies and voluntary agencies. Are voluntary organisations little more than just another service provider? It has made many people think about the future development of their organisations – how do we retain an independent view and a critical voice when operating within a contract culture? It has also raised a whole host of organisational, legal and managerial issues for trustees and managers of voluntary organisations to grapple with.

The themes of this book

This book does not argue a position one way or another about whether voluntary organisations should or should not enter into contracts with public sector bodies. Instead it has three main themes.

1 To emphasise the need for all parties to understand fully the nature of the changes involved in negotiating and managing contracts.
2 To clarify the ideas, terminology and approaches involved in the contracting process (including a distinction between how they are meant to work and how they often operate in practice).
3 To help voluntary organisations identify how they can take a proactive approach to contracts rather than allowing the other party to set the agenda and determine the pace.

It is important to recognise that there is no single model or uniform approach to contracting. In some areas individual organisations have managed the process with little understanding of the services for which they are contracting. They have used and only slightly adapted the techniques used by public authorities to buy in other services or commodities. In other areas contractual relationships have been developed over a number of years as the conditions around grant aid have become tighter.

The work involved in bidding for and managing contracts is not a new feature for many organisations; for years they have had to bid for work, deliver services to an agreed standard and criteria and manage a series of expectations and demands from different stakeholders. However, contracting requires an increased level of organisational and managerial clarity and competence.

Features of traditional grant-aid relationships

A useful learning point is the difference between the traditional arrangements and more recent contractual arrangements set up between voluntary organisations and statutory bodies.

There is a range of definitions of the status of a grant, but most suggest that a grant is given freely by the donor on the understanding that the recipient will use it well to further the purpose of the organisation.

The traditional relationship between a statutory body such as a local authority and a voluntary organisation was one of grant aid. There was often little explicit direction on how the grant was to be used – the main sanction possessed by the donor was the threat of *not* giving future grants.

Grants made by statutory bodies to voluntary organisations often have the following features:

Voluntary organisations seen as 'on the fringe'
The main work was carried out by statutory organisations in house. Local councils and the NHS ran their own services and employed their own staff. Voluntary organisations filled the gaps by organising extra or niche services or by campaigning for better services.

Annual funding
Most grant-aid arrangements were for one year. Although some grants were renewed on a regular basis, grants have increasingly become project based or fixed term.

Grants to aid the organisation
Grants were a mechanism to encourage and sustain an organisation. The grant paid for or contributed to the running costs of the organisation so that it could then do 'good things'.

Paternalistic relationship
In some places the process of allocating and giving grants was a highly subjective one. Often public authorities expected a certain level of control and influence in the management of the organisations they funded.

Little direct monitoring
The monitoring of grants was often done on a fairly 'light touch' basis. The emphasis was on showing that the grant was being spent, or on measuring activity rather than results.

Features of contractual relationships

A contractual relationship has the following features:

Voluntary organisation as delivery partner
The focus is on delivery. The organisation is contracted to provide a service that is needed and can be measured. The service it delivers links into the statutory organisation's priorities or plan.

Longer-term or often fixed-term funding
Some commissioners have moved away from short-term programmes. There is some recognition that year-to-year funding causes uncertainty, is time consuming and makes planning and development hard. Contracts are often for a longer period.

Contracts as a binding agreement
Contracts are legally binding agreements with clear expectations and obligations on *both* sides and have stricter enforceable remedies if the contract is breached.

Arm's-length or business arrangement
The relationship between the parties should operate in a business-like way. Both parties need to respect each other's role and interests. It should be recognised that both partners are independent and are responsible for managing their own affairs.

Emphasis on measurement and outcomes
Most contracts include a requirement to produce regular monitoring information to show that the contract has been properly delivered and that standards have been met. Increasingly there is an interest in producing evidence of outcomes (what difference or change the service made) as opposed to a simple record of the activity or output.

Contracts for specific services or clients
Grant aid usually funded an organisation or a project. Contracts tend to be more specific and focused on the delivery of a service to a defined client or community.

VAT
Most contracts are regarded by the tax authorities as requiring the supply of a service to the funder; the supply of services is in many cases subject to VAT.

Approaching contracts

Managing the 'cultural shift'

On reflection we failed to realise the cultural shift involved in moving from grant to contracts. We focused too much on the legal and managerial issues involved in drafting contracts – things like insurance requirements, bidding timetables and so on. We overlooked some of the bigger changes in roles and relationships.

In the authority we still have not really worked out what we mean by commissioning. We were comfortable about directly managing and running services, but all of the changes involved in identifying future user needs, managing the market, outcome evaluation and developing choice are still being talked about. It is a whole new way of working for us.

For our voluntary sector colleagues I think that they need to appreciate that a contract relationship is significantly different from a grant-aid one. We saw grants as a way of supporting the sector. A contractual relationship can and should be a collaborative partnership, but we need to feel confident that the organisation is able to deliver targets and maintain a consistent and reliable standard of service.

Senior local authority manager for adult care

What is driving the move to contracts?

Several factors have combined to encourage voluntary organisations to take on a much greater role in delivering public services. Some of the key factors regularly quoted include:

Emphasis on working together

In the past agencies often worked in isolation. There was often poor communication and rivalry between services. Government has put great emphasis on 'joined-up government' and partnerships between sectors. As the government's 2006 White Paper on local government put it: 'We want the best local partnership working between local authorities and the third sector to be the rule, not the exception, and for the sector to be placed on a level playing field with mainstream providers, when it comes to local service provision.'[1]

A strategic and thoughtful process of commissioning

A major development in the management of public services has been the emergence of a commissioning role. Commissioning should include all the activities involved in assessing current and future needs, consulting with service users and designing and securing an appropriate service. Commissioning should be a strategic and thoughtful process. It should be much more than simply finding the cheapest supplier and ticking the boxes to ensure that the supplier delivers the specified service on time.

Economic gains

Traditionally, when faced with a need or demand or with a legal duty, public service organisations (PSOs) have usually set up their own service organisation and employed their own staff to deliver these services. The past two decades, however, have seen whole services go out to competition; such services are eventually delivered by either private sector companies or other independent agencies such as voluntary organisations. There is an assumption that contracting services out can bring economic gains and free up PSOs to take a more strategic view rather than be involved in the detail of managing a service directly.

Enhanced role for the voluntary sector

The voluntary sector is being encouraged or expected to play a much greater role in society. Voluntary organisations come in many shapes and sizes. The sector is now a significant employer in many localities and is often the key local expert.

---

[1] *Strong and Prosperous Communities – The Local Government White Paper*, DCLG 2006

A belief that voluntary organisations can offer more

The government needs a voluntary and community sector that is strong, independent and has the capacity, where it wishes, to be a partner in delivering world-class public services. To help achieve this, the government will increase funding to build capacity in the sector and increase community participation.

Comprehensive Spending Review, 2002

There is a view that voluntary organisations can add more to a service. The use of volunteers, an organisation's local roots and its credibility with the community can add extra value to the core service.

An Audit Commission study in 2007[2] identified three main reasons why government and commissioners want to encourage contracting with voluntary organisations:

1 Voluntary organisations operating alongside public and private sector providers can make for a larger, more diverse and more competitive supply base for public services.
2 In some service areas, voluntary sector organisations may have a particularly good understanding of users' needs or a distinctive delivery capability. This is likely to produce high-quality services, well targeted to the specific needs of diverse groups of service users.
3 A healthy voluntary sector can make valuable contributions in a local area beyond the delivery of public services, notably to public participation, social inclusion and community engagement.

Several commentators have suggested that the main driving force behind voluntary organisations having a much greater role in public service delivery is the perception that they will do it more cheaply or that by contracting a service out to an external agency the public body can also transfer risk or any difficult management responsibilities.

The five prerequisites of successful contract management

The move to contracts usually generates a lot of work. A new vocabulary of words such as 'specification', 'preferred bidder' and 'performance indicators' has to be learnt, services have to be defined, costed and measured and bids have to be written.

However, in the midst of the detail there is a real need to think and act strategically. As a result of our research for this book we have identified five prerequisites that organisations need to have in place if they choose to enter into contracts.

1 Early involvement in the process

All too often voluntary organisations are 'bounced' into the contracting process. Commissioners require bids to be submitted with ridiculously short deadlines. Credible organisations that could deliver a service are overlooked, are not invited to bid and not included in the process.

Managers need to invest time in building effective working relationships with relevant commissioners and purchasers before the contracting process shifts into gear. They need to ensure that their organisation has a good profile with commissioners and also that their organisation and its users are able to play a positive role in influencing commissioning practice and priorities.

---

[2] *Hearts and Minds: Commissioning from the voluntary sector*, Audit Commission July 2007

2 Clear strategic thinking and planning

It is easy, and at times tempting, to sit back and let the statutory sector run the whole process. This can only lead to an entirely reactive approach. It is therefore important to develop a shared view within the organisation about the contractual role and an agreement about how it is to develop.

A good strategic planning process that involves all the key people should help an organisation to develop a sense of purpose and a strong sense of identity. This should in turn enable it to:

- work out the kinds of contracts and partnerships with which it wants to be involved
- identify how the organisation fits with other agencies.

Doing this can help the organisation to develop some clarity about its specific role and the potential for cooperation with others.

3 The development of a diverse business model

There is an obvious risk in being dependent on one or two main income sources. A change in policy or direction, or a disagreement in the relationship, can put an organisation's future in jeopardy. Often organisations find themselves in a position where most of their income comes from one or two main funding sources. Over time, organisations need to build a business model that creates a wider mix of income sources. This reduces risk, helps to create independence and prevents an organisation becoming totally reliant on one main funder.

4 The creation of strong values

Values are the principles, ethos and key organisational beliefs that should hold an organisation together. Values might cover issues such as how people should be treated, the status and rights of users and other core philosophies. Values are what the organisation stands for rather than what it does. Strong and clear values can help trustees and staff navigate their way through a series of decisions such as 'should we bid for this work?' and 'is it in line with our values?' Clear values can help an organisation say 'no' to inappropriate or potentially incompatible projects.

5 Implementing sound organisational processes

The contracting process tests an organisation's internal management and systems. An organisation needs:

- the information, processes and skills to cost services and projects accurately and fully
- to understand the legal and managerial issues of taking on a contract
- to be able to write realistic bids that are successful.

These processes take time and can put pressure on managers and trustees. All are manageable but they may require some investment and external support.

Thriving in the contract culture

The extent, character and practicalities of contracts between voluntary and public sector agencies will vary from place to place. For some it will be a challenging and demanding process; for others it will be the logical next stage in their organisation's development. Four factors seem to be critical in being able to manage and thrive in the contract culture successfully.

1 Identify opportunities and engage in the process

Managers and all those in leadership roles need time away from day-to-day operational matters to identify opportunities, decide how to engage in the process and evaluate results.

2 Maintain a strong sense of independence

No one can *force* a voluntary organisation to enter into a contract. Voluntary organisations are not (or should not be) just another service provider. They can legitimately play other roles such as campaigner, innovator and advocate. It needs to be appreciated that voluntary organisations play different roles.

3 Be confident about your organisation's value

Often people in voluntary organisations fail to recognise or show the real value they add or the real difference they make. The outcomes they deliver or contribute to and the expertise and skills built up in the organisation are either taken for granted, overlooked or ignored. Contracting requires the organisation to be confident and assertive about recognising its strengths and ability to make a difference.

4 Show willingness to take the initiative

There is a tendency to let the commissioner completely design, control and manage the contracting process. This creates a position in which the voluntary organisation can only react to or fit in with the contracting process. An alternative approach is to invest time in influencing what gets contracted, lobbying and pressurising for best practice and working with other organisations to ensure that they do not become isolated.

Funding mechanisms

There are several types of funding relationships possible, ranging from open-ended grants to competitive tendering. All have opportunities, issues and risks.

	Open-ended grant	Specific grant	Service contract	Contract for specific projects or clients	Open competition for the contract	Independent agencies take over a service run by a statutory body
Description	A grant 'donation' from a statutory body to encourage and support the work of a voluntary organisation.	Still called a grant, but with specific expectations set.	A formal agreement to support the organisation.	The organisation is contracted to deliver to specific clients.	The statutory body invites organisations to bid to deliver a service on an open or pre-selected basis.	A statutory body transfers the management of a service to an independent agency and pays a fee for it.
Example	A district council votes to give an annual grant of £8,000 to support a charity-run day care centre.	A council provides a grant to deliver a project offering home care support to older people.	A service contract is negotiated between a charity and a social service department to deliver a range of services to older people.	A charity is contracted to provide home care support for individual clients referred by social services.	A charity bids against other private and voluntary providers to run a contract to support older people.	A charity takes over the management of a local authority daycare centre.
Issues	Often very loose. Awarded annually. Hard to measure.	As more conditions are added it often starts to resemble a contract.	Block funding. Framework agreement.	Does the contract fee cover the full cost of delivering the service?	What criteria are used? Who gets invited to bid?	Transfer of employment. Service management risk.

What sort of relationships are possible?

The following seven items describe the kinds of relationships that can exist between voluntary organisations and PSOs. The focus is on the character of the relationship. How would you describe the ones that your organisation has?

Type	Description	Issues
1. Funded as a good cause	The organisation is seen as a good cause to be supported.	■ Usually as a grant. ■ Emphasis on funding the organisation.
2. A partnership	The organisation works alongside the statutory agency to achieve a clear and shared outcome.	■ Collaboration. ■ Working together. ■ Sometimes vague and ill defined.
3. Part of the consultative and policymaking process	The organisation is regularly involved in helping to formulate policy and future strategy.	■ Meets a need to show that the public bodies have consulted. ■ Can be time-consuming work – which is often not directly paid for.
4. A provider/supplier of designated services	The organisation is seen as any other supplier – it delivers a pre-determined service under contract.	■ Business relationship. ■ Emphasis on performance delivery, value for money and management.
5. The voluntary organisation represents a key interest group	The organisation is seen as representative of a significant interest group or stake.	■ Way of working with hard-to-reach groups. ■ Danger of tokenism.
6. A niche or specialist agency	The organisation is recognised as having a particular expertise or providing a very specialist service.	■ Recognition that the organisation has the expertise and resources to deliver a specialist or unique service.
7. A longer-term investment	The public agency invests in the organisation to build its capacity in the hope of future gains.	■ Funding to build up capacity to deliver in the future. ■ Funding as an investment.

Approaching contracts

Valuing what we do

When our manager first started talking about bidding for contracts my heart sank! We have kept this organisation going using a mixture of grants and fundraising for 20 years. At times it has felt a bit hand to mouth, but we have just about survived. Contracts felt like a very new and demanding ball game.

It did mean having to raise our game. For the first time we had to work out what each service really costs. It also made us think about what services we did and did not want to run in the future. It also made us stop and think and review our activities and strategy.

Possibly the biggest gain has been recognising that most of our services deliver real change and make a lasting difference for communities. They are as good as, if not better, than other providers that sometimes cost a lot more.

As a result we have been a lot more assertive with the two statutory bodies that we work with. We have taken the initiative in showing them evidence that our work is making a difference. In the past, we went "cap in hand" and almost apologised for asking for grants. Now our approach is to show the value of our work and see ourselves as a credible and effective player.

Treasurer, community project

All about contracts

To a large extent the shift from grants to contracts over the last 15 years has been about changes in funding mechanisms to align the funding of voluntary organisations to PSOs' objectives. This is particularly true with regard to small and medium-size organisations. Relatively few local voluntary organisations have been involved in bidding for contracts competitively.

Grant aid was the traditional way of funding voluntary organisations. It came with conditions but these were often simply around ensuring an annual report and accounts were submitted to the grant-making body and the grants were viewed as being there to support the organisation to do 'good work'. Little was said about how the money should be spent, but as organisations developed services to meet the needs of their members and users, organisations pointed to these as a reason for increased funding.

With the advent of the purchaser and provider split in the late 1980s, councils and parts of the health service looked to the voluntary sector to see if there were ways in which it could take on more of a provider role. They also wished to formalise the arrangements of existing provision. One way of achieving this was to convert grant arrangements into 'service level agreements'. Often this simply took the form of writing up the organisation's existing grant-aided activities and services in the form of an agreement. Some monitoring measures were usually included (mainly output based) and, generally, business carried on as usual.

In some cases (mainly in adult social care) provision that had previously been provided by the local council or health authority was put out to contract. Relatively few of these were contracts that voluntary organisations bid for competitively; most were the result of an agreement that the voluntary organisation was best placed to provide the service. However, the funding mechanism for delivering the service was now that of a formal contract with specific outputs identified as being required in return for payment.

Contracts today

Over the last five years there has been an increase in the number of contracts going out to tender. Often these have been for new service developments and have offered a way for organisations to expand.

In a few high profile cases existing contracts have been put out to competitive tendering, resulting in one voluntary organisation winning the contract against another voluntary organisation.

If this has been the landscape over the last 15 years, what's new or different about the current situation? There are a number of drivers.

- European Union procurement rules and principles.
- The development of a national strategy on public procurement.
- The quest for value for money.
- The desire of central government to improve public services (and in some cases to cut costs) and its belief that in order to do this it needs to work in partnership with the private and voluntary sectors.

Whilst much of the contracting with voluntary organisations in the past has been about changing the funding mechanism for existing services and purchasing new services (procurement), the government now seeks to encourage local public bodies to commission services from the voluntary sector alongside mainstream providers.

The legal context
There can be confusion about what a contract actually is, particularly where service level agreements are concerned.

What is a contract?
A contract is any legally binding agreement. Contracts are not legally required to be in writing – they can be made orally, electronically (by email or by ticking an 'I accept' box on the internet) or by an exchange of letters.

The following are important features of a contract.

- Each party has to agree to do something and gets something in return (i.e. the 'consideration'). Intention to create a binding legal agreement is essential. Whilst not all mutual promises create a contract, most will do so and in the business context (i.e. the offer to provide certain services for a certain amount of money) the intention to create legal relations will almost invariably be present.
- The existence of a 'consideration'; a consideration is anything of material benefit but in the context of service contracts it will normally be money paid by the funder and the services provided by the recipient.
- The contract is created when the offer is unconditionally accepted. Withdrawal of an offer is always possible until it is unconditionally accepted.
- Organisations need to ensure that, when making a bid, they are not accidentally[3] making a contractual offer, which would then become binding upon them if it were accepted.

Commissioning principles for public service organisations

In *Partnership in Public Services*,[4] the Office of the Third Sector defines commissioning as the entire cycle of assessing the needs of people in a local area, designing appropriate services and then securing them.

It goes on to outline the following commissioning principles for PSOs:

- Develop an understanding of the needs of users and communities by ensuring that, alongside other consultees, they engage with third sector organisations as advocates to assess their specialist knowledge.
- Consult potential provider organisations, including those from the third sector and local experts, well in advance of commissioning new services, working with them to set priority outcomes for that service.
- Put outcomes for users at the heart of the strategic planning process.
- Map the fullest practicable range of providers with a view to understanding the contribution they could make to delivering these outcomes.
- Consider investing in the capacity of the provider base, particularly those working with hard-to-reach groups.
- Ensure contracting processes are transparent and fair; facilitating the involvement of the broadest range of suppliers, including considering sub-contracting and consortia building where appropriate.
- Seek to ensure long-term contracts and risk sharing wherever appropriate as ways of achieving efficiency and effectiveness.
- Seek feedback from service users, communities and providers in order to review the effectiveness of the commissioning process in meeting local needs.

---

[3] For further information see Chapter 3 'The Process'
[4] *Partnership in Public Services: An action plan for third sector involvement*, Office of the Third Sector, 2006

'Intelligent commissioning'

The Audit Commission, in its report on commissioning from the voluntary sector,[5] endorses these principles as a framework for what it identifies as 'intelligent commissioning'. At the same time it argues that these principles are not particular to the voluntary sector but apply whether commissioners are buying services from the public, private or voluntary sectors.

Its report goes on to state that these principles should not imply preferential treatment for the voluntary sector but that the pattern of commissioning should be characterised by 'competitive neutrality' between different service providers (i.e. a commitment to a level playing field between public, private and voluntary sector providers of goods and services).

The elements of intelligent commissioning are defined in the report as follows:

- sound understanding of user needs
- well-developed understanding and management of markets
- good procurement practice which comprises: the choice of funding approach (grant or contract); the process prior to awarding the grant or contract; the basis for determining price; and, post award, the effective management of the working relationship.[6]

An approach based on intelligent commissioning has much to offer the voluntary sector both in providing more opportunities for bidding for services and in contributing to the design of services to meet user needs.

However, there is no standard approach to public procurement. Each PSO will have developed or be in the process of developing its own internal procurement rules and procedures.

Nine ways to influence commissioning

- **1 Start early**
  To be effective in influencing commissioning, organisations need to start early, before decisions to contract have been made and before specifications have been drafted.

- **2 Be involved in strategy**
  Increasingly, commissioners are seeking input into their strategy and forward plans. This can be a useful way of shaping future agendas.

- **3 Involve users**
  Often voluntary organisations can open up a dialogue between service users and commissioners. This can be an opportunity to feed back user experience and talk about needs and expectations.

- **4 Identify trends**
  It is useful to record trends in the changes affecting a service and its users. Feeding back trends about patterns of use, changes in the sector and new demands can open up a discussion with commissioners.

- **5 Link up with government targets**
  Often commissioners are under pressure to show that their services meet centrally-driven targets or policies. It is useful to show commissioners how an organisation can help the commissioner meet these demands.

- **6 Record gaps and unmet needs**
  Having systems for recording and analysing gaps in provision or occasions when an organisation has not been able to meet public or user needs can be a valuable source of information. Collating evidence of gaps and unmet needs can help to feed into future plans.

- **7 Share experience**
  Joint training events, project visits and other forms of exchange can be ways of helping commissioners to keep in touch with the realities faced by staff delivering services.

[5] *Heart and Minds: Commissioning from the voluntary sector*, Audit Commission July 2007
[6] See Figure 1, Appendix 1, 'Intelligent Commissioning'

Nine ways to influence commissioning (continued)

- **8 Produce evidence**
  Developing evidence that a service creates a lasting and sustainable outcome can be a strong message for commissioners. Case studies, user feedback and evidence from third parties can all be used to describe successful outcomes.

- **9 Participate!**
  See involvement in consultation meetings, inter-agency partnerships and other networks as an investment. Although time consuming, they can be an opportunity to meet commissioners, raise your organisation's profile and influence thinking.

The language of a contract

The last decade has seen a plethora of terms added to the vocabulary of voluntary organisations. The following table lists a selection of them with their definitions as used in this book. Some of the words may of course have different meanings in other contexts.

Term	Description
Added value	Benefits you offer beyond the contract specification.
Approved list	List of suppliers/providers to which the tender document will be circulated, those suppliers having met the pre-determined criteria, usually by completing a pre-qualification questionnaire (see p.14).
Asset transfer	The transfer of buildings or other physical resources from the public sector to another agency, either on a temporary or a permanent basis.
Best value	The process central government required local authorities to implement in order to ensure that they were providing services in the most efficient way.
Bid	A formal proposal to supply goods and services outlined in the service specification and usually outlining how the contract requirements will be met.
Commissioning	The process of assessing the needs of people in a local area, designing services and then securing them.
Compact	A memorandum concerning relations between the government and the voluntary and community sector expressing a commitment to working together for the betterment of society.
Community interest company	A legal structure available for social enterprises to set up limited companies which are designed to ensure community benefit.
Contract	A binding agreement to provide services or goods in exchange for a consideration (usually money).
Contract notice	A notice published in the *European Journal* announcing a public service organisation's intention to put out a contract for goods or services and explaining the process by which this is to be done.
Contractor	The person or organisation that enters into a binding agreement to provide services or goods in return for a consideration (usually money).

All about contracts

Term	Description
E-auction	An online tendering process where bidders bid against each other live to offer the lowest price.
Evaluation	The process of assessing bids against pre-determined criteria in order to select the best one. OR Reviewing an organisation's process and programme against its original needs and objectives.
European Journal (OJEU)	The *Official Journal of the European Union*, where all contract notices for Part A services (see Chapter 3) must be published for tenders that fall within the European procurement laws. The contract value thresholds above which such contracts must be published are laid down in EU Directives.
Framework agreement	An arrangement where a purchaser selects the supplier and fixes the terms and cost for a period in advance (usually three years) and the supplier delivers as and when required.
Full cost recovery (FCR)	Covering all the costs of providing a service, including relevant overheads.
Inputs	The resources allocated to a particular activity.
Indicators	A tool for measuring an aspect of a contract's performance.
Invitation to tender (ITT)	A formal letter from a public service organisation to a provider inviting it to submit a tender for a particular service. The ITT will usually include the specification for the contract and the instructions for the process and may also include the terms and conditions that will govern the contract once it is active.
Impact	The longer-term change and difference achieved by undertaking a particular activity.
Milestones	Key pre-determined objectives that indicate what has to be achieved in order for a project or activity to be successful.
Monitoring	The collecting of information about a service in an organised way.
Output	A type of performance measure indicating the deliverables of a project or service, usually by volume (e.g. number of clients, number of queries).
Outcomes	The effect, difference or changes that a service or activity makes or influences.
Partnership	A cooperative relationship between people or organisations that agree to work together and take shared responsibility to achieve a shared goal.
Performance measure	A pre-set measurement that reports on a specific aspect of performance of the contract.

All about contracts

Term	Description
Pre-qualification questionnaire	A questionnaire used by public service organisations to check the suitability of suppliers and providers and shortlist the ones they will invite to tender.
Procurement	The process of buying goods and services from an external agency.
Provider	A supplier of goods and services.
Public service organisation (PSO)	A public organisation that provides and/or manages government and public sector services.
Purchaser	The buyer of goods and services.
Quality service	One that is consistently fit for purpose, responsive to users and performs to agreed standards in the contract.
Quality assurance	The organisational process by which quality standards are agreed, managed, monitored and improved.
Risk analysis	An assessment of the risk to an organisation of bidding (or not bidding) for a contract. Risks being assessed could include financial, organisational, legal, credibility or political.
Social enterprise	A business that trades with a social purpose using business tools and techniques to achieve social aims. Some social enterprises operate as independent provident and mutual societies; more recent social enterprises have set themselves up as community interest companies.
Service level agreement	An agreement between a public service organisation and voluntary organisation to provide a range of services. Sometimes described as a 'soft' contract.
Specification	A description of the services to be delivered under contract.
Sub-contractor	A person or organisation contracted to fulfil part or all of another's contract obligations.
Tender	A written proposal outlining how a supplier would deliver and meet the requirements outlined in a service specification and the price it would charge.
Two envelope	A two-stage tendering process where bids are first evaluated on technical and quality factors where the purchaser only looks at the price (in the second envelope) if the technical and quality criteria are met.
TUPE	Transfer of Undertakings (Protection of Employment Regulations) is the legal protection given to employees whose employment is transferred from one business to another.
Value for money	An audit of the economy, efficiency and effectiveness of a service either by making comparison with similar services or by measuring the cost of not doing something.

The different types of contract

There is a range of ways in which PSOs can contract with the voluntary sector to deliver services.

The table below lists the most common and gives examples of how they are frequently used. Some agreements can incorporate more than one type of contract.

Type of contract	Description	Examples
Unit purchase or spot contract	A contract is issued as and when the service is used or client placed.	A training programme receives a fee for each trainee who joins a course. A hostel is paid for each occupied bed.
Time-based contract	An agency is paid to deliver X amount of a service to a client or a community.	A carers' organisation is paid to provide 100 hours of home care support per week. An advice agency is contracted to provide a helpline for 20 hours a week.
Project contract	An organisation is paid a fee to start up and manage a specific contract.	A health charity takes on a two-year fixed-term contract to train school nurses to deliver sex education.
Block agreement or service level agreement	A single agreement to run a range of activities and services.	A community centre is awarded a contract that covers all of its main activities.
Outcome-based contract	A contract linked to a specific result or change.	A training programme is funded on the number of clients achieving a particular standard. An agency is contracted to reduce antisocial behaviour on an estate.
Management contract	An organisation is contracted to be the managing agency of another provider.	A local Council for Voluntary Services provides the management support and legal framework to enable a community group to run a local health promotion campaign.

Voluntary organisations need to pay attention to the type of contract they enter into. Some contracts are more suitable for particular services than others. For example, organisations need to be careful about payment by numbers of clients where they rely on other people referring to them; if the service relies on a certain number of referrals being made then that needs to be made explicit in the contract.

Many organisations have been used to having a block agreement with their purchaser. These arrangements are likely to come under much closer scrutiny than previously as PSOs develop their commissioning process.

The process of contracting

Public sector procurement is the purchase of goods and services by a public service organisation (PSO). PSOs include;
- central government departments (e.g. Department for Children, Schools and Families, Department of Health, Home Office, Learning and Skills Council, National Offender Management Service)
- the National Health Service and primary care trusts
- local authorities, universities and colleges.

Legal background

The European Union (EU) Procurement Directives set out the legal framework for public procurement. They apply in those circumstances where public authorities are required by law to invite tenders when entering into new contracts with service providers. These Directives have been implemented into UK law by the Regulations,[7] which came into force in January 2006.

The purpose of the EU procurement rules is to open up the public procurement market and ensure the free movement of goods and services within the EU. They set out procedures which must be followed before awarding a contract where its value exceeds set monetary thresholds. The Directives reflect the government's procurement policy, which requires that all public procurement must be based on value for money (VFM). This is defined as the optimum combination of whole-life cost and quality to meet the user's requirements, which should be achieved through competition unless there are compelling reasons to the contrary.

Public service contracts are classified in the UK Regulations revised in January 2006. These Regulations implement the European Union Procurement Directives, which are discussed above.

Service contracts are classified as Part A services or Part B services. Examples of Part A services include computer support, financial services, management consultancy and market research. Part A services are subject to the full EU procurement regime. These services have been identified as being the type of services that are of most interest to service providers from other member states in the EU. Part B services include recreational, cultural and sporting services, social services and health care, and educational and vocational health services. Only limited procurement procedures apply to Part B services.

Part A and Part B services both have a value threshold, over which the Regulations apply. The threshold for Part A is currently 137,000 euro and for Part B 211,000 euro.[8] For Part A services any contract notices over the threshold must be published in the *Official Journal of the European Union* (OJEU). This does not apply to Part B services. Part B services are considered to be generally of less interest to service providers from other member states.

If a PSO is purchasing a mixture of Part A and Part B services and supplies in one contract (a mixed contract) then it will be subject to the rules of the greater part – the one with the higher value.

---

[7] *The Public Contracts Regulations 2006*, The Stationery Office
[8] Current levels as set out in *The Public Contracts Regulations 2006*, ibid

Types of contracts awarded by PSOs

PSOs can award three types of contract:

Services

Most voluntary sector organisations' services are in the fields of health and social services, education and training, all of which are classified as Part B services. Most of the rules will therefore not apply to them. Significantly, the rules that relate to the obligation to hold a competition, the criteria to be applied and the tender process itself, do not apply.

Supplies

Supplies contracts involve the purchase, lease, rental or hire purchase of goods or products and include vehicles, computer software and educational material.

Works

Works contracts are broadly construction related and will not apply to most voluntary organisations.

The four principles governing public procurement

Even when a tender process is not subject to the Directives (e.g. because the contract value is below the relevant threshold) the EU Treaty governs all public sector procurement contracts in the UK and establishes four fundamental principles which govern public procurement:

1 *Equal treatment*
   Suppliers are entitled to fair and equal treatment at every stage of a contract award procedure.
2 *Transparency*
   Information about contracts and rules to be applied should be available to all interested candidates. The rules that will be applied in assessing applications for tender lists and the criteria for selection should be clearly advertised.
3 *Proportionality*
   The demands placed on the providers should be both relevant and directly related to the contract being awarded.
4 *Mutual recognition*
   This requires that the standards, specifications and qualifications in use throughout the EU receive equal recognition to ensure services are suitable for their intended purpose.

In line with the principle of transparency, the European Court of Justice has recently ruled that:

- all public contracts must receive an appropriate level of advertising which enables the services market to be opened up to competition
- the impartiality of any procurement process should be reviewed.

This is likely to have an impact on local authorities seeking to award Part B service contracts.

Opening up the services market to competition is also in line with the UK government objective of achieving value for money in *all* public procurement contracts, not just those covered by procurement directives.

Best value and 'the four Cs'

In local authorities 'best value' is providing an additional spur to open up the services market to competition, based on 'the four Cs':

- **Consult** – users and the public, to see what they think of what is provided.
- **Compare** – provision with other alternatives and provision in other areas.
- **Challenge** – the basis on which something is done: is there a better way?
- **Compete** – could better value be obtained by opening up the market to competition?

In addition, all PSOs are under pressure to implement the government's agenda in reforming the way public services are delivered to achieve better outcomes.

Engaging with the commissioning process

There is no standard approach to public sector procurement. Each PSO will have developed its own internal procurement rules and procedures, based on the three levels of regulation: at EU, national and local level. Most purchasing of services from small to medium-size voluntary organisations will be at local level and governed by internal standing orders, by-laws, financial regulations, local strategies and policies.

The reality is that many public authorities are going beyond what is required by the Regulations. The Regulations themselves do not necessarily impact on many tendering processes for services provided by the voluntary sector. However, if a public authority wants to use a tendering process, there is nothing to prevent it doing so and it can be a good way to ensure best value. It is likely that individual public authorities will have their own rules requiring tendering, and the challenge for voluntary organisations is to engage effectively with whatever tendering process is in place.

Stages in the commissioning process

A formal commissioning process would normally include the following stages:

Identification of need

A definition of aims, what is needed (a service specification) and the business case.

Making the decision to outsource

A decision as to how the procurement process will be carried out. The decision will take account of market conditions, legal obligations and public sector policies.

Requesting expressions of interest/pre-qualification questionnaire

There may be a pre-qualification stage that suppliers are asked to go through before being asked to make a bid. This is usually a questionnaire asking for evidence of financial status, experience, references, etc.

Circulation of invitation to tender (ITT)

The PSO asks your organisation to put in a bid. The ITT includes all the arrangements for the bid, including a timetable and the formal arrangements for complying with the tender. It will usually include a draft copy of the contract terms and a list of criteria which will be used by the PSO to assess the bid.

Evaluation of tenders against specification and the pre-determined award criteria

The PSO assesses all the bids against its pre-determined criteria. This can include a presentation by each supplier.

Contract awarded

The PSO announces who it will award the contract to and arrangements for unsuccessful bidders to get feedback on their bids.

Contract negotiation/agreement

Everyone involved works together to put things in place for the contract. Some areas of detail may need to be negotiated.

Contract management

The successful organisation and the purchaser manage the contract; performance against the contract specification is monitored and reviewed by the purchaser.

The focus of the European Directives is very much on a tight procurement model for goods and services and some PSOs reflect this in their tendering process. However, there has been recognition from the government that to deliver its public service agenda it needs third sector organisations to be involved with the whole commissioning process and not simply as contractors.

Commissioning frameworks

A number of government departments are already engaged in creating or updating commissioning frameworks that set out the principles of how commissioning should be developed, offer examples of best practice and, in some cases, set standards for taking commissioning forward. In particular the Communities and Local Government is working with stakeholders to create a framework (through statutory guidance) for local government by April 2008.

In addition, the government has committed to training public service commissioners to help them give the third sector a greater role in the design and delivery of public services.

National and local compacts

Public sector purchasing from voluntary and community organisations is also subject to the terms outlined in the National Compact and individual local compacts. The Compact (see page 26) is an agreement between the government and the voluntary and community sector. Its principles include recognising that groups are independent and that they have the right to campaign even if funded by government. Local compacts often outline the terms of engagement for contracting between local PSOs and local groups.

Experience at local level

Whilst much of what has been said at a national level is reassuring to the voluntary sector, the experience at local level is much more mixed and the picture is very much one of a transition period. Some local authorities have moved to a very tight procurement policy – in excess of the requirements of national legislation but as part of their own value for money/best value reviews – and have decided to put out existing service level agreements to tender. This has triggered much anxiety, particularly amongst smaller groups where the contract value is very low (and started as a grant) but is nonetheless vital for the continued existence of the organisation.

Influencing the commissioning process

Some primary care trusts and local authorities are taking a longer view of commissioning and using the change to look at existing services, analyse need, consult users and providers and map out the market rather than simply tendering existing services.

For voluntary sector organisations the challenge is to try to engage effectively at the early stages of the process and to influence it. This involves recognition that your organisation may not be seen as the automatic choice for user feedback. Many public authorities have, over the years, changed and improved the ways in which they consult with the public.

Part of the challenge for voluntary organisations is coming to terms with the fact that they don't have an automatic right to provide a service. Many commissioners (and indeed many users) are not particularly interested in who delivers the service as long as the service itself is good. This means that organisations must be proactive and take responsibility for finding out how commissioning will work in their area and how the organisation can influence the process effectively.

Influencing the process

Identify what sort of power and influence base you have: expertise, credibility, independence, access to users, resources or knowledge, access to users/clients.

Find out how the system works: needs identification, service planning, gaps and trends identification, commissioning process, contract process.

Clarify interests and priorities: what is driving their plans; accountability and targets; national directions; hidden agendas.

Agree outcomes: start at the outcomes, establish common interests, link the work into their strategy, distinguish between ends and means.

Build relationships over time: use their language, build different relationships, stress added value, talk about more than funding – collaboration, partnerships and investment.

The choice of procurement procedure

For those contracts covered by legislation, the choices are as follows:

1 **The open procedure**
   Under this procedure all those who show interest and respond to the advertisement are invited to tender.

2 **The restricted procedure**
   A selection is made of those who respond to the advertisement based on economic and technical information provided by suppliers and only they are invited to submit a tender for the contract. This allows purchasers to avoid having to deal with an overwhelmingly large number of tenders.

3 **The competitive dialogue procedure**
   The authority enters into a dialogue with bidders following an OJEU notice and a selection process to develop one or more solutions for its requirements and on which chosen bidders will be invited to tender. This is designed to cope with particularly complex projects such as public-private partnership projects.

4 **The negotiated procedure**
   Under this procedure a purchaser may select a number of providers with whom to negotiate the terms of the contract. The purchaser must invite at least three bidders to negotiate the contract, where there is a sufficient number of suitable providers to select. Again, this is used in more complex projects and where there may be more than one solution that meets the requirements.

Public authorities have a free choice between the open and restricted procedures. The competitive dialogue procedure is available where the contract cannot be awarded under either of these procedures. The negotiated procedure may only be used in the very limited circumstances outlined in the Regulations.

Most contracts for local voluntary and community organisations are awarded under the restricted procedure. An early meeting with the procurement officer of a PSO can be an invaluable way for an organisation to obtain information, both in order to influence the process and to understand the procedures that will need to be followed in order to be successful.

Getting onto the tender list

For many voluntary organisations the reality of the new situation is that they will move from a situation where they have in effect been the preferred supplier (i.e. the purchaser has decided that no other suitable provider exists and has awarded/renewed a contract on that basis) to an open or restricted tender. It is therefore vital that voluntary organisations:

- find out what is happening in their area
- ensure that their names appear on any 'invitation to tender' lists
- sign up to email alerts for new contracts.

Filling in questionnaires

In some areas questionnaires have been sent to all current providers and they have been asked to complete a declaration of interest for the areas of work they are able to provide.

Some organisations will have been asked to complete a pre-qualification questionnaire which aims to establish whether the organisation is 'fit for purpose'; if so, it will then be placed on the list from which the public authority will invite tenders. Any pre-qualification questionnaire will need to be widely advertised to ensure that all potential providers can complete one and therefore have an equal opportunity to go on the list.

Some public authorities include the 'fit for purpose' tender questionnaire within the tender pack itself. It helps the PSO to evaluate whether a provider is able to do the work on basic criteria such as status, financial standing, health and safety policy, environmental policy, equal opportunities policy and experience of delivering the services. It also assesses the organisation's technical capacity and ability to meet the fuller brief and the suitability of the organisation to participate in the tendering opportunity.

The invitation to tender

An invitation to tender will typically contain the following:

Introduction/introductory letter	Explains why tenders are being invited and gives some background to the service.
Service specification	Sets out what the successful bidder will be required to provide.
Tender timetable and arrangements	This will set out all instructions for completing the tender and the timetable including any key stages (such as a selection interview) and how to obtain further information.
Financial and contractual arrangements	A draft copy of the main terms and conditions of the contract with which you will be expected to comply.
Tender evaluation criteria	A list of criteria which explains how the bid will be assessed.
Tender questionnaire	If you have not completed a pre-qualification questionnaire this will be included in the tender pack: standard questions asked of all tenderers to check out experience, operational arrangements and financial standing.

At the stage of filling in the tender questionnaire, you need to remember that it is incumbent on you to meet all the arrangements and deadlines for submission exactly. Some invitations to tender will include self-addressed envelopes which must be used to return the bid. The invitation may state the number of hard copies required. If you do not fulfil such requirements it is likely that your bid will be ruled as non-compliant and be disqualified from the process.

When a formal tendering process is *not* used

A formal tendering process is *not* used when:

- Either no bids or no appropriate bids were received in an open or restricted tender process.
- There is only one supplier that can deliver the requirements.
- For technical or artistic reasons or for reasons connected with the need to protect exclusive rights (e.g. the intellectual property rights attaching to the service required) only one supplier can deliver the contract.
- There is a need to proceed urgently due to unforeseeable events (except where these events are attributable to the PSO).
- There is a need for repeat or additional works, supplies or services, which must be provided by the original supplier (e.g. for reasons of compatibility).
- Contracts are of a low value and therefore it is not deemed cost effective to go through a formal tendering process.

Electronic procurement

Some public procurement processes may require voluntary organisations to engage with online based procurement. Here, the most likely procedure is that PSOs carry out all or part of the tendering process online.

Usually an interested supplier receives an email notice to go to a website to download an invitation to tender. The site will include all the supporting documents. Suppliers then submit bids by going back to the website to lodge their completed tender.

Evaluation of the tender

The tender will be assessed by the PSO on pre-set criteria and a shortlist of tenderers may be invited to a selection interview.

Tenders are often evaluated in two stages.

- The first stage ensures that the technical specifications are met and that the product or service will meet the specification and performance requirements.
- The second stage is evaluation. If a tender does not meet the requirements it will be rejected. Pre-published award criteria cannot be altered.

An announcement of the winner of the contract will then be made. This will be the provider whose bid offered the best value for money as set out in the pre-published criteria. If the contract is for Part A services and is over the threshold (currently 137,000 euro) there must be a standstill period of 10 days to allow unsuccessful tenderers to seek further information about an award decision and enable them to take action in the courts if they feel they have sufficient grounds. In most cases the standstill clause will not apply and unsuccessful tenderers will be written to informing them of the outcome and setting out arrangements for debriefing/feedback on the bid.

Everyone involved with the successful bid then works to put everything in place for the contract; issues of detail within the contract should be negotiated before the contract is signed. It is therefore crucial that your organisation does not bid unless you are certain you can meet the terms of the contract.

What happens if things go wrong?

Some voluntary organisations have felt that they have been or are being 'squeezed out' by PSOs when it comes to contracting out services and that they are not properly taken into account when discussions are taking place around commissioning.

It is important to understand that public authorities, as public bodies, have obligations in the form of various public law duties. These run alongside any private law commitments, such as those set out in contracts. Voluntary organisations can use these obligations to make their voices heard.

There are four areas which public authorities need to consider when they are putting services out to tender.

1 **Consultation**
   In certain cases they have a duty to consult. They must give consultees sufficient information and time to comment on their proposals. The consultation must take place when the proposals are at a formative stage and the results of the consultation must be taken into account when the public body makes its decision.

2 **Transparency**
   Public bodies must act fairly and they should give reasons for their decisions. There should be transparency and openness in their decision-making and they must not be, or appear to be, biased. When making a decision, a public body must take into account all relevant information.

3 **Procedures**
   If a public body predetermines issues or does not follow the set procedure for making a decision it could be found to be acting unlawfully.

4 **Legal powers**
   A public body must not act beyond its powers. Whatever a public body does it must be able to point to some legal provision which permits it to act in such a way.

Judicial review

A judicial review enables a court to look at how a public body has behaved and decide whether it has acted lawfully and fairly. If it has not, the court will then decide whether to order the public body to take its decision again, in a fair and lawful way. Judicial review can also stop the clock running on any imminent action by a public body whilst a decision is challenged by applying for 'interim relief', which ensures that the public body must maintain the status quo until the proceedings are concluded.

Procurement decisions are often held not to be subject to judicial review unless there has been bad faith or a special public law element (for example if the local authority has not followed its standing orders). Public bodies have a considerable amount of freedom in deciding who to award a particular contract to, as long as the process is fair to all parties.

Successful judicial review

In 2004, service users of Voluntary Action Leicester and five other local voluntary sector organisations sought a judicial review of Leicester City Council's decision to stop funding them, as they did not provide core services.

In 2003 the council decided it only wanted to fund what it called 'core services'. It reviewed the work of the voluntary sector and then wrote to the relevant groups saying that their funding would run out at the end of the financial year when current grants ran out. The groups were given 28 days to comment. The council had not told the groups what 'core services' meant nor why they were considered not to be providing them. The error was compounded by its failing to explain why groups that had been providing 'strategic or statutory services' during the last review (only two years previously) were now facing closure.

The judge found in favour of the service users. In his view, once the consultation process started it had to be fair. It was unfair in this instance because the council did not explain what 'core' meant. This was a criterion for deciding ongoing funding which had never effectively been put to the groups. The judge pointed to earlier legal cases that said consultation must take place when a decision is still at a formative stage; those consulted must have sufficient information to give the proposals intelligent consideration and a reasoned response; the results of the consultation must be taken into account by the public body.

The judge thought that the groups had been treated so unfairly that the council should be forced to make its decisions about funding again, using a new and fair process which included explaining the criteria 'clearly and comprehensively'.

Unsuccessful judicial review

A decision by Hammersmith and Fulham Council to reduce funding to a local law centre from £261,000 per year to £102,000 was upheld after a challenge by three residents failed.

The three claimants argued that the council's procedures had been flawed because it had acted too quickly, leaving no opportunity for representations to be made; the council had given no reason for its decision.

However, the judge said that if the law centre had been unhappy with the process it should have challenged from the outset and should not have sent the council a 70-page application form explaining how it met new criteria. He found in favour of the council and ordered costs against the claimants for the council's written defence.

The Compact

The Compact (see page 26) may provide the basis for a public law challenge, as there is an overlap between the Compact codes and public law principles. However, the Compact itself is difficult to enforce as many public bodies do not take it seriously and there are no sanctions for non-compliance.

Challenges under EU regulations

A service provider that has suffered a loss as the result of a breach of the Regulations can enforce these rules against a public body by taking it to court. Before bringing a case to court the service provider must tell the public body of the breach and its intention to bring a claim under the Regulations. Any claim must be made within three months from the date the grounds for the claim arose.

Breach of contract

A procurement process may give rise to an 'implied contract' between a public body and the tenderers. It is unclear how far this type of contract would extend but there may be grounds for a claim if a tenderer has been unfairly excluded from the process if it has not been conducted fairly by the public body. A claim can only be pursued in these circumstances if some loss actually results from the breach.

What does this mean for voluntary organisations?

Legal remedies are very limited. Some successful challenges have been made but these have usually been to do with the process rather than the decision made.

It is very difficult to challenge the outcome of a tendering process as long as the process itself is fair. At local level a local authority has a very wide discretion as to what it funds and how. There is no duty to fund the voluntary sector as such, and as long as a decision is taken lawfully (following a fair process) it could in theory stop funding all projects altogether.

Key questions about the tendering process

- Has the public body consulted properly and disclosed all the relevant information?
- Have you been given the time and information to make a proper response?
- On what basis has the public body decided to use a tendering process?
- Do the Regulations apply?
- Is the tendering process fair and is it being operated fairly towards all tenderers?

The Compact

The Compact between government and the voluntary and community sector sets out a series of principles and undertakings to develop the relationship between government bodies and the voluntary sector.

The National Compact includes Codes of Good Practice – on black and minority ethnic groups, community groups, consultation and policy appraisal, funding and procurement and volunteering. These cover rights and responsibilities which government, local public bodies and the voluntary and community sector should reflect in their relationships to make them work.

Local Compacts are agreements between local government, local public bodies and the voluntary and community sectors. Most local authority areas are now covered by a local Compact.

Compacts are usually based on the following principles:

- Voluntary action is an essential component of a democratic society and an independent and diverse voluntary and community sector is fundamental to the wellbeing of society.
- Government and the voluntary and community sector have distinct but complementary roles in the development and delivery of public services.
- Partnership working adds value.
- Voluntary organisations are entitled to campaign within the law in order to advance their aims.
- Good practice in grants and contracts.
- The importance of promoting equality of opportunity.

Several local Compacts have also included supportive statements around full cost recovery and developing fair practice in contracting.

The Compact can be a useful reference point for ensuring fair and good practice throughout the contracting process.

Analysing an opportunity

An organisation's involvement in contracting can come about in a number of ways:

- existing arrangements are firmed up and converted into a contract
- a commissioner contacts organisations that it has already approved as potential providers and invites them to bid for a contract
- a commissioner advertises that it wishes to seek bids from potential providers
- a commissioner makes a direct approach to an organisation and invites it to make a bid.

Responding to a contract opportunity

Deciding if and how to respond to a contract opportunity is an important decision in any organisation. It means considering a range of issues and factors including:

- your organisation's capacity and ability to meet what is being asked for in the specification
- the potential risks involved in taking on the work.
- the extent to which the contract is achievable and realistic for the costs involved
- the relevance of the contract to your organisation's purpose, values and strategic direction.

It is important that your organisation is well prepared and organised in its approach to these issues, as deadlines from commissioners often demand a quick response. Your organisation needs to appoint a person who can authorise a bid for a contract and agree the criteria by which a contract opportunity should be evaluated and considered.

> *I have learnt not to underestimate the work involved in making a bid for a piece of work. By the time you include all the work in preparing costings, writing the tender and attending meetings, I estimate that we spent something like five staff days on a recent bid for a relatively small contract.*
>
> *Manager, health project*

What is in a specification?

A specification should be a full description of the service or activity that the commissioner intends to purchase. It should contain the following:

1. **Background**
   Some commentary on the level of need, how the service was identified and what might be the commissioner's purpose in establishing it.
2. **Aims or intended outcomes**
   What is the service meant to achieve.
3. **The scope of the service**
   Who is the service for?
4. **Description of services to be provided**
   What kind of service will the successful provider have to deliver?
5. **Service expectations**
   A description of the policy, practice and standards to be applied by the provider.

6 **Contract details**
   The commissioner will probably indicate the intended length of the contract, key terms and how much it anticipates paying for it.

7 **Process and criteria for bids**
   A guide setting out what providers need to do if they intend to make a bid. This will usually specify the information potential providers will have to supply, the format they should use to bid and the timescale for making bids.

Evaluating a specification

Service specifications vary considerably as to how specific they are. A useful grid for analysing specifications is shown below.

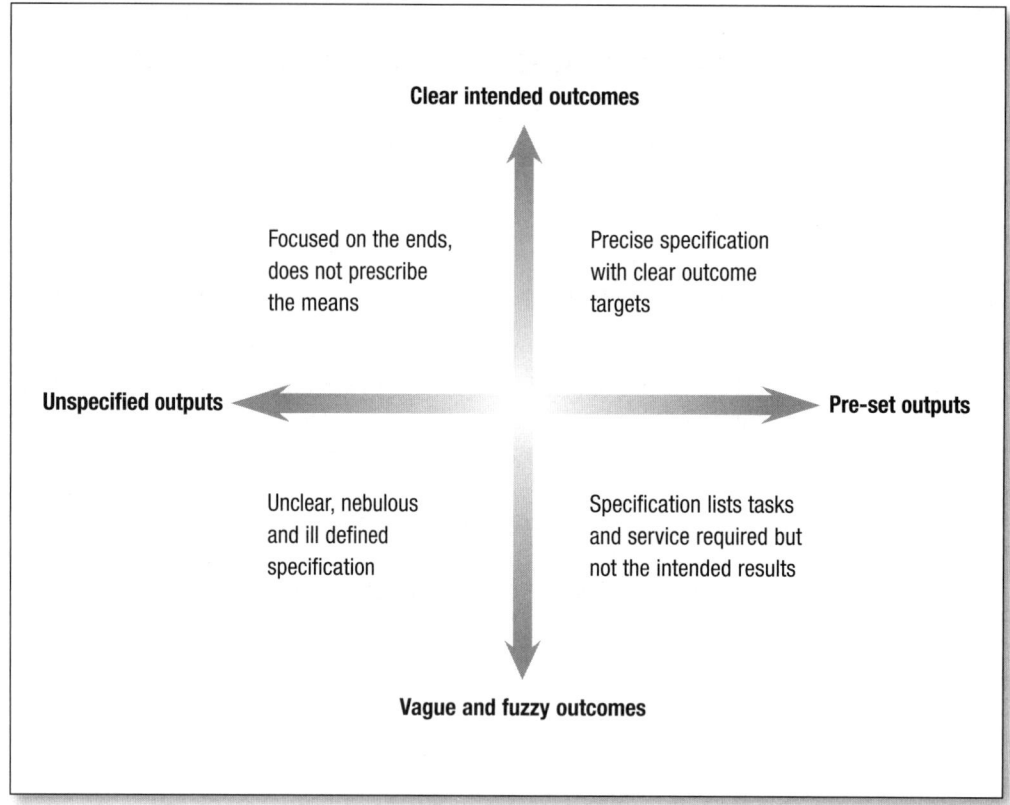

Analysing an opportunity

	Description	Example	Issues	Questions to ask
Focused on the ends; does not prescribe the means	The commissioner sets out the intended outcomes. The bidder has to come up with a service plan and approach that will meet the outcomes.	The aim is to reduce truancy from local secondary schools by 20 per cent in two years' time.	Difficult to cost and plan. It is for the bidder to show that its plan of work will achieve the outcomes.	Who has set the outcomes? Are the outcomes really what service users want and need? Are the outcomes achievable and sustainable in the time available?
Precise specification with clear outcome targets	The commissioner sets out in the specification what they want to achieve and how they expect the provider to do it.	The aim is to reduce truancy from local secondary schools by 20 per cent in two years' time by developing an inter-agency programme and delivering an awareness campaign.	The commissioner has a very clear idea of what it wants and what it expects the provider to do. Is there a risk of a lack of flexibility? Is the provider really just a sub-contractor or agent of the commissioner?	Is there any room for flexibility? Are the prescribed outputs likely to deliver the intended outcomes?
Unclear, nebulous and ill defined specification	The specification lacks clarity or detail about the intended purpose of the service or what the provider will do.	The authority intends to commission a service to reduce school truancy.	The specification lacks any real detail. It is more a 'request for proposals' whereby bidders suggest what they think needs to be done. Does the authority really know what it wants? Often driven by resources or policy: 'we need to be seen to be doing something' or 'we have to spend £x by …'.	How would the commissioner measure success?
Specification lists tasks and service required but, not the intended results	The specification is output focused. It details what the provider must do and deliver, but is vague about the intended outcomes.	The authority seeks providers able to deliver 30 hours per week of outreach work.	Is there a need to clarify the intended outcomes? Might there be a better way of achieving the outcomes?	Is the commissioner open to alternatives?

29

Specifications vary considerably in style, length and format. Some are highly defined descriptions of what is needed, whereas others are much broader, open requests for proposals. Some are focused on describing the kinds of outcomes commissioners want to see and leave it for providers to show what they would do to deliver them. Others are much more prescriptive and set out in detailed terms the kinds of service outputs that the successful provider will be required to deliver.

Analysing a specification

In analysing a specification it is useful to focus on the following questions.

What has led to the decision to invest in the service?

It is worthwhile to try to find out what assumptions lie behind the service and what has led to the decision to invest in it. Some might be quite clear, for example:

- **Pressure to meet national targets**
  Increasingly, local public bodies are being held accountable and are required to show that they have met nationally set standards or targets.
- **Meeting a political or strategic objective**
  A new service might arise from a policy commitment made by politicians or senior managers. It might come from their personal interest and vision to create a new service.
- **Response to pressure from users or communities**
  The specification might be a result of lobbying and pressure from users, potential users or other concerned groups.
- **Response to external funding**
  The authority might have been successful in winning special grants from central government.
- **The need to manage or invest in the market**
  Commissioners might have identified gaps or under-provision in services. The specification might be an opportunity to introduce more choice into the market, or to meet an unmet need.
- **Past service failure**
  Current or past services might have been identified as failing by inspection agencies, managers or users. Going out to contract might be the way of starting again and drawing a line under past shortcomings.

Other factors influencing the decision might be less clearly stated, or part of a hidden agenda, for example:

- **Need to try something innovative**
  The commissioner wants to find a new way of tackling an issue.
- **Need to test or demonstrate something**
  By contracting out a pilot project a commissioner can test out an idea and show it works.
- **Need to meet a target or goal**
  The emphasis is on delivery. The commissioner has clear targets that it has to meet and believes contracting may help to achieve them.
- **Need to respond to a need**
  The commissioner has to show that it is responding to need.
- **Need to bring in skills and expertise**
  The commissioner lacks the skills and expertise to deliver the service inhouse.
- **Need to be seen to be doing something**
  The commissioner is under political pressure from management, external inspectors or communities to deliver something.

- **Need to off-load a problem or risk**
  The current arrangements do not work or are perceived as having too many risks. Contracting it out could transfer the problem.
- **Need to spend budget**
  The threat of underspend. The commissioner has to spend its budget before a set time.

To what extent have potential users been involved in drawing up the specification?

Increasingly, commissioners are trying to find ways of involving and consulting users in deciding what should be commissioned. Such attempts to involve users in service design, setting standards and planning improvements are still at a relatively early point. Often user involvement is slow to take off and has to overcome a history of not involving and ignoring their experiences and aspirations. Many organisations lack the skills and processes to engage users actively.

It is useful to check that the intended service, as described, is what users actually want rather than what commissioners believe they might need. It is also worthwhile to check that the diverse needs and expectations of potential users have been taken into account. One size may not fit all. Often organisations might engage with only a handful of individual users and from that dialogue believe they have something called a user point of view.

Is the service achievable?

This is a critical judgement. Can the service really make a difference? As commissioners increasingly talk about delivering outcomes it is important that a potential bidder is confident that achieving the desired outcome is realistic, achievable and within its capabilities to deliver as a provider.

Are there any hidden agendas?

Often some expectations or issues are held back. It is easier to write a specification that covers quantifiable factors that relate to volume of delivery, opening hours and service output, for instance. Some factors, such as relationships with other partners, profile and other considerations, are harder to specify, but are often critical in determining the success of a service or project.

Locally, we have one senior commissioner for both the primary care trust and local authority, which works very well. There are no separate agendas to play to and the process is very transparent. We have built up good relationships locally over the years and established our organisation as an expert in the field and a reliable provider. We have actively involved ourselves in strategic planning groups and have been invited to be part of the local implementation team. Our organisation feels confident that whatever the changes locally, the commissioners will consult properly and ensure that the voluntary sector will be able to compete on a level playing field.

Manager, local health charity

Ten questions to ask about a specification

1. What's the background to this specification?
2. How clear are the intended outcomes?
3. What risks are involved?
4. What must the service deliver?
5. What is needed for this service to be a success?
6. Who has a stake in this service?
7. What is the current position?
8. Why has the public body decided to go out to contract?
9. Is it what users really want?
10. Is it realistic?

What assumptions are inherent in the specification?

In any management or planning exercise assumptions are made about how things will be. By analysing the specification it might be possible to identify the assumptions that are built into the service specifications. Examples of assumptions include:

- level and extent of demand for a service
- the likely cost of resources to deliver a service
- the levels of cooperation and support available from other agencies
- the time needed to achieve an outcome.

A potential provider should be confident that the assumptions are logical and sound and if successful it is prepared to go along with them.

Often commissioners will invite potential providers to clarify points before submitting a bid. Some commissioners hold briefing meetings for all potential providers. Such events can be a useful opportunity to develop a feel for the thinking behind the specification. They also ensure that all potential bidders receive the same information and hear consistent answers to questions.

Identifying the risks involved in taking on a service

All initiatives, activities and services involve an element of risk. Risk assessment is the process of being clear about the potential risk involved, assessing the likelihood of the risk occurring and planning what to do to prevent or manage it if it does occur. Risk assessment involves making any risks clear from the start and being confident that the level of possible risk arising from an activity is acceptable and reasonable.

The possible risks of taking on a contract

Business risk

Costs might be hidden or may rise sharply. The cost of managing the contract might be much greater than anticipated.

Delivery risk

The levels of demand for the service might be much greater than anticipated. Being involved in this kind of work might open the way to potential litigation.

Credibility risk

Failure in this area might badly affect the reputation of the whole organisation.

Internal organisational risk

Key and experienced staff leaving would prevent the contract being delivered. Taking on this kind of work might pull the organisation into other areas of work and change the focus.

Political risk

Changes in the council might lead to new priorities and a new direction. Will support still be forthcoming?

Sustainability risk

What happens after the three-year contract? Users will still have needs: will expectations be placed on the organisation to continue something for which there are no resources?

Discussion about risk needs to be objective and clear-headed. A good way to test risk is to develop future scenarios by asking 'what if...?' questions. The purpose of the exercise is not to eliminate any potential risk by taking on activities only if no risk is present. Rather it is to ensure that board members and managers know what they are taking on and are willing to live with that level of risk.

The relevance of the specification

An important issue is how the proposed service would fit with your organisation. Several issues need to be considered here.

1 Legal capacity
The governing document of a charity sets out the purpose of the organisation, its powers and the area of benefit. Such a clause puts a limit on the kinds of issues an organisation can take on. Your trustees need to be satisfied that they have the legal powers to take on a contract.

2 Strategic direction
It is easy for an organisation to be pulled in several different directions at once. Jumping at opportunities for funding can distort an organisation's future direction. The service you are considering should be in line with the stated direction or plan for your organisation.

3 Values base
Organisations need to be clear about what they stand for and see as principles. Values frequently involve issues of how users are respected and treated. Taking on a piece of work that might be based on a different set of values or a different ethos could lead to your organisation losing its independent identity and possibly to conflicts with other parts of the organisation.

4 Organisational capacity
An organisation can only take on a limited number of new activities at one time. It is important to check that your organisation has the space, management time and resources to take on the contract. It is also important to check that you have the skills and expertise necessary to deliver the contract properly.

5 Fit with the organisation
It is important for you to make sure that the new service would complement the other activities and services that your organisation currently runs.

CASE STUDY

Learning to say 'no'

Helen, the manager of the Morton Health Centre, assumed that her organisation's management committee would simply 'nod through' a decision to put in a bid to the local primary care trust (PCT) to run a two-year health lifestyles project aimed at the over-fifties. The idea for the project had been developed by a group of health workers and it was felt that the health centre was the logical place to run it.

After a brief introduction, the committee started to challenge the idea. At the previous month's centre away day everyone had agreed that the key priority for the centre was to work with young people. Taking the health project on would pull the centre in another direction. The centre's treasurer was concerned that taking on another project would stretch its administration even further. There was also concern that a two-year project would not really give enough time to do anything meaningful and could simply raise demand and expectations. The organisational cost involved in starting up a new activity that would last for only two years was not seen as proportionate.

As the discussion continued Helen could see that the consensus was not to bid. This caused her some concern – if they turned this down would the PCT invite them to bid for other work?

After the meeting, Helen met the commissioning managers at the PCT. They were initially surprised at what she had to say: it was the first time any voluntary organisation had turned down funding! Helen explained how the centre had reached its decision.

In the longer run, Helen now believes that this decision has in fact strengthened the centre's reputation with the PCT. 'They see us as being quite focused and unwilling to drift. Turning down an opportunity was a new thing for us. It's not how we usually operate! But it has enabled us to define our identity and show that we really are committed to our planned direction.'

Analysing an opportunity

Making the decision to bid

The decision to bid for a contract needs to be taken in an informed and detached manner. All too often the pressure caused by urgent deadlines and the need to 'get the work' has led to organisations bidding for work that is inappropriate, under-costed and not in line with their purposes.

A valuable exercise is to develop a list of criteria to use when considering whether to bid for new work. Such an exercise can be a useful part of your organisation's business planning process. These agreed criteria offer managers a means of evaluating opportunities and ensuring consistent decision-making in the organisation.

CASE STUDY

Bid criteria – an example

A voluntary organisation developed these criteria to evaluate all specifications that it was considering bidding for:

Criteria	Issues to check
1. Is it in line with our value base?	Does the commissioner share our ethos and service principles?
2. Is it what users want?	Have potential users been consulted about the specification?
3. What could be the impact on reputation?	Will this service enhance our reputation and identity?
4. Is the contract financially viable?	Does the proposed fee fully cover our costs? Are there any hidden costs?
5. Are the contract terms fair and reasonable?	Is the timescale reasonable? Is the balance of risk fair?
6. Do we have the capacity to do it?	Do we have the relevant skills and expertise to do this work? Do we have the organisational capacity to take this on and successfully manage it?
7. Is the level of risk acceptable?	Are the organisational, business and other risks acceptable to us?
8. Does it fit with our strategy?	Is in it line with the direction set out in our agreed business plan?
9. Is it sustainable?	Can adequate arrangements be made to ensure that work continues after the contract period? Can we develop an exit strategy?

The organisation's Assistant Director commented, "It was a very useful process to draw up the criteria. Some of the issues are absolutely essential – they are deal breakers. We would not bid if they were not covered. Others require negotiation and judgment.

"It is interesting in the past how we have often bid for work and taken on projects that were underfunded, not properly thought through and even outside our remit. We were inclined to be funder-led and jump on whatever bus was passing!

"Having some criteria means that managers and trustees can manage the process and ensure that we are in control of what we bid for."

5 Making a bid

Elements of a successful bid

A **bid or tender document** needs to convey several different messages. It needs to convince commissioners that your organisation is capable of successfully delivering the service described in the service specification. It should highlight your organisation's experience and competency, and persuade commissioners that, compared with other bidders, your organisation has a winning edge.

Making a successful bid involves several elements:

1. Analysing and understanding what is needed.
2. Identifying what your organisation can bring to it.
3. Costing and pricing.
4. Writing the document.
5. Being asked to do a presentation or interview about your bid.

It is important to be aware that your bid is more than a funding proposal. In the event of a dispute the acceptance of a tender bid to a specification could be regarded as a binding agreement – so the statements, pitch and terms proposed in the tender could be regarded as creating a binding contract.

Some bid processes are strictly governed. Tenders have to be submitted in a precisely defined way and answer very precise questions. Others are more open ended, requiring bidders to pitch their ideas on a blank piece of paper. The work involved in putting a bid together can be considerable and needs to be seen as an investment cost in an organisation.

Analysing and understanding the bidding process

Here is a simple model of what makes up a purchasing decision, involving potential purchasers evaluating three items: the price, quality and reliability of the provider.

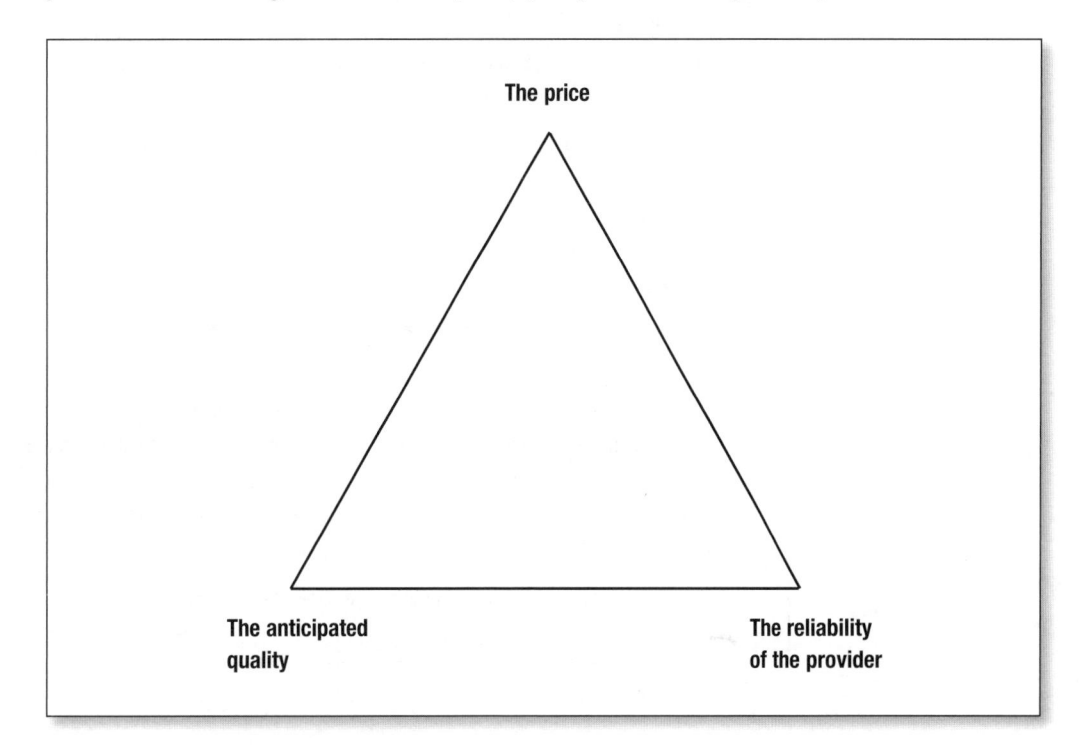

```
                    The price
                       /\
                      /  \
                     /    \
                    /      \
                   /        \
                  /          \
                 /_____\
         The anticipated   The reliability
            quality         of the provider
```

Price
The price is often the most tangible and certain element of the bidding process. The purchaser may indicate in the contract specification how much it expects or is prepared to pay for the service. Or the provider has to cost the service and then decide how to price it.

Quality
The quality factor can be made up of different elements. Some aspects are about hard quality, such as whether the service meets pre-set standards. Other elements relate to more human or 'softer' factors such as how users feel about the service.

Reliability
The reliability element relates to the capacity and experience of the intended provider. Does it have a track record? Does it have the people, systems and processes to manage the contract properly?

Quality assurance systems

In some sectors of the economy, having a recognised quality assurance system is an essential prerequisite for any contract bid. Quality assurance systems usually involve the setting and recording of key standards, defining how the organisation should work and what users should be able to expect.

The most common national systems are:

Practical Quality Assurance System for Small Organisations (PQASSO)
PQASSO is a quality assurance system designed specifically for use within voluntary and community sector organisations. It is based on self assessment. PQASSO covers 12 quality standards and promotes continuous improvement through self assessment. PQASSO is managed and developed by Charities Evaluation Services.

ISO 9000
ISO 9000 (previously known as BS5750) is a quality management system. The focus of ISO 9000 is on the consistency and operation of an organisation's working systems and practices. Emphasis is placed on having all working systems fully documented. External assessors will then review the system.

Investors in People
Investors in People is a national standard which sets out a level of good practice for the training and development of staff in order to achieve business goals.

Organisations apply to be assessed against 10 key best practice indicators which form part of the Investors in People standard. If the external assessors can find sufficient evidence of policy and practices in line with each indicator, the organisation is awarded 'recognition' of its Investors in People status.

National networks
Various national networks such as Citizens Advice and MIND have developed their own sets of standards to which their local members must adhere.

Some commissioners are attracted to using national standards as a way of assessing quality and the reliability of a bidding organisation's management. Others are willing to allow organisations to demonstrate that they have developed their own systems and standards for quality. There has been some concern that ISO 9000 is mainly focused on documenting procedures and systems (the assumption being that if the systems are right, the user will get a good service) and not on what users want and regard as quality.

It is advisable to establish early in the process if a commissioner intends to insist on a particular quality system.

What does the commissioner really want?

The specification for the bid you are making should give you some indication of what is important in each of the three elements and also how each element will be tested.

Often a specification only tells half the story, however. It is easy to be specific about the details of a service such as volume, opening times and other outputs but rather harder to define such factors as user engagement, user experience and outcomes. It is useful therefore to try to test what the commissioner really wants; investing time in researching circumstances and background and following up opportunities to clarify issues with commissioners might give you some clues as to what is really required as opposed to what the formal specification says is needed.

Identifying what your organisation can offer

A good bid has a distinctive feel to it. It should highlight the organisation's particular expertise and strengths. Often voluntary organisations are faced with two problems: (1) it's not part of the organisation's culture or style to market itself or be assertive about its strengths, or (2) the organisation lacks evidence to back up claims of successful work.

A worthwhile exercise is to try to assess your organisation's strengths against known or potential competitors. Possible factors to compare might include:

- experience
- approach or service model used
- location
- relationship to users
- organisation
- style
- background
- ethos

A thorough analysis of the competition will indicate your organisation's distinctive or unique strength, its unique selling proposition (USP).

Potential competitor	Its strengths	Its weaknesses	What it can offer	Cost/price issues	Quality	Reliability	Issues for our bid
XYZ charity – a local voluntary agency doing similar work	Locally based. Well established.	Seen as old fashioned.	Low cost. Been around for years.	Probably doing it on the cheap.		Safe but dull.	Need to show that our service model is up to date and at the leading edge.
Slick – a national charity keen to develop local services outside of London	National brand.	No local contacts. It is 'parachuting' into the area.	National reputation.	Its costs must be high as it has to pay for a national infrastructure.	Loads of paper systems.	Strong.	Stress our local links and that we are in touch with local users.
Timos – a newly established social enterprise	New start up – full of promise.	Not proven.	Unknown – it is bidding for everything to get work in.		Not tested.	No track record.	Highlight our established reputation and that we are a dedicated local specialist.
Unity – the social care division of a housing association	Good organisation.	This isn't its core business – it's a new departure.	Already has contracts with the authority.	Probably more expensive than us.	Not much user involvement.	Good reputation – a safe pair of hands.	Could we work with it? Should we talk about a joint venture?
Network – a private company	It has had similar contracts in other areas.	Poor training record. High staff turnover.	Strong on marketing.	Cannot see how it can run this contract and make a profit out of it.	Mixed – some bad reports.	Not sure that it has invested in the infrastructure.	Stress our training programme and good rates of staff retention.

Recording evidence of good work

The staff of voluntary organisations know that they do good work and make a difference, but their organisation often lacks any effective mechanism to record this. Over time, organisations need to become more effective at identifying and collecting evidence of their work. Such evidence can be very valuable in the bidding process. Being able to refer to evidence will allow you to avoid your bids containing empty and immeasurable slogans such as 'we deliver a quality service' or 'our service makes a difference'.

Possible sources of evidence of good work might include:

- independent evaluation reports
- feedback from service users, ex-users and agencies that refer clients
- evidence of changes or progress in clients as a result of your work
- evidence from third parties who may have observed change.

Collecting such evidence together can help to highlight an organisation's strengths and identify issues to highlight in the bid. It also means that the organisation has an evidence base should a potential commissioner decide to probe any of the claims made in a tender bid.

Added value

An economist would define 'added value' as being the stage when the value of the original input is increased (i.e. made more valuable) due to work or process applied to it. A cook, for instance, uses his or her skills and experience to add value to the ingredients to make a meal.

Voluntary organisations often claim that through their work they add value to a service or project. Often the added value elements of an organisation's work can be more than simply 'extras'. Added value might include:

- generating or recruiting additional resources (e.g. other funding, volunteer time) to add to what the contract brings in
- using knowledge, skills and experience to improve the reach, delivery or quality of a contracted service
- using resources that are already in the organisation to manage, develop or improve the service.

Added value can give a tender bid a valuable edge over other bidders. It is therefore important that you recognise and make claims for your organisation's added value. The manager of a voluntary sector children's project commented:

> *It took me a while to come to terms with the idea of added value, but once I did I saw several elements of it that surprised me. For example, the staff team are often asked to provide consultancy advice, input into policy meetings and lead training sessions for local authority staff. It is not part of our service contract. It's quite incredible how much we 'give away', without reward and recognition. We are happy to carry on doing it, but want some recognition of it. I also highlight possible added value in bids and in contract monitoring exercises.*

Examples of added value

- An organisation recruits, trains and supports volunteers to provide additional support and personal mentoring to service users. The work carried out by the volunteers is not one of the outputs of the contract, but makes the core service more personalised and valuable.

- By being part of a national network an agency is able to share ideas, use its resources and develop best practice. This means that a local agency has a national perspective and as such its services are continually improving.

- An organisation developed evaluation and monitoring systems to identify changes in need, spot gaps in services and show user experience. Although not part of the contract, the organisation regularly used this information to help commissioners develop their future service strategy and plans.

- A community organisation argued that as it was well established in the local area it stood a greater chance of being able to reach out to potential users. It had credibility and was well known locally. Previous projects had given it an understanding of the different networks that existed in the neighbourhood and access to a range of community leaders who would help to market the project. It would take a new organisation a long time to build up such knowledge and credibility.

- As a charity an organisation was able to raise extra income from charitable and public sources. This income was used to develop social activities for its residents and improve recreational activities, thus making the core service more accessible, sociable and valuable for residents.

- An organisation working with people suffering from a long-term medical condition was able to argue that as all of its management committee members and most of its staff had either cared for or suffered the condition, this gave the organisation a level of knowledge that would ensure that services were relevant to the user group.

Costing and pricing your bid

Working out how to cost a bid is more than a numbers exercise. It involves the use of accurate data or making a best guess about the different potential cost elements in a service, identifying what it will cost to manage and support the activity and then deciding how to price it.

Over the past few years there has been some considerable concern about costing for contracts, particularly over:

- reluctance from funders and commissioners to meet the full cost of a service
- the perception that by using voluntary effort or by raising charitable funds voluntary organisations can deliver a service at a cheaper rate than other providers
- lack of accurate information about what a service really costs – traditional budgets were often very general and not designed to give precise information
- a culture in some organisations of being unwilling to ask for the full cost of a service in the belief that it will be rejected.

All departments should ensure that the price of contracts reflects the full cost of the service, including the legitimate portion of overheads.

HM Treasury, 2002 cross-cutting review

Making a bid

> **CASE STUDY**
>
> ### At what cost?
>
> The finance manager of a children's charity described her organisation's experience of costing services:
>
> 'Three months after I took over in this post, I carried out a review of some of the key contracts and compared the actual cost of running the service or project with the costs schedule anticipated in the bid. I then looked at them again on a full cost recovery basis.
>
> 'It was a very revealing and alarming exercise. It was obvious that we had failed to properly cost many of our contract bids. Several of the ones that we had won we were propping up and internally subsidising. We never knew the extent to which we were doing this!
>
> 'We have had several discussions about this with our management team and with our trustee board. A lot of my colleagues were quite shocked at what services really cost. We are not a cheap option.
>
> 'A lot of my work as finance manager is making sure that managers properly cost bids and don't take on projects because of guilt or with vague plans to raise money from elsewhere to support them. It means that at times, I have to be very unpopular.
>
> 'We had an interesting debate about taking on work below cost. We recognised that there are certain occasions where we will never get a fee to cover the full cost.
>
> 'There is a whole range of difficult or unpopular causes that we support. If the work is of a high priority to us, fits with our mission and is of an innovative nature we might take it on. For example, we have just taken on a project working with the children of travellers – a group that is quite hard to get funding for. We have agreed to come up with about eight per cent of the project's full cost. We see this as our investment in the project. We are trying to get the purchaser to operate as a joint venture or partnership between them and us. We have to put very strict limits on how much we will put into it. Although the occasions when we take on services that are loss making will be rare, we now at least have some processes for identifying the real costs. In the past, we never really knew what things cost us.'

Full cost recovery: the ACEVO/NCP format

A study by the Association of Chief Executives of Voluntary Organisations (ACEVO) reported that between 2003 and 2005 one third of ACEVO members were forced to close down services due to financial insecurities caused by a failure to cover the full costs of operating a contract.

In 2004 ACEVO published *Full Cost Recovery: A guide and toolkit on cost allocation* in partnership with New Philanthropy Capital (NCP). It introduced an approach to costing services that is increasingly being used throughout the sector and acknowledged by funding bodies as a logical process.

At the heart of full cost recovery is the idea that in any organisation there are two types of costs: the direct costs of delivering an activity and the indirect costs of supporting the delivery process and managing the organisation.

The ACEVO/NPC format divides organisational costs into four categories:

- **Direct output costs**
  Direct output costs are the dedicated costs involved in delivering the service. They are the costs involved in employing staff and resources that directly deliver or work with the service user.
- **Direct support costs**
  Direct support costs are the costs involved in supporting and supervising the service delivery. Time involved in supervising project workers would be included here.
- **Indirect support costs**
  Indirect support costs pay for the organisational functions that provide a base for services to be delivered. This would usually include central management and administration, finance and facilities. They are not directly involved in the service delivery.

- **Governance and strategic development work**
  Governance and strategic costs cover the costs of meeting regulatory functions and costs involved in developing future activities for the organisation.

Our experience of full costing was interesting. We developed a format similar to the ACEVO model. What is interesting is the surprise factor involved in finding out what something really costs. We have a contract to provide a youth service to a rural community. The direct costs of the service are relatively small – mainly the costs of employing two part-time youth workers who deliver 20 hours per week of local youth work. When the service was tendered for we added on an eight per cent management cost to cover the overheads. The figure of eight per cent was plucked from the air. However, the costs involved in managing the workers, providing good supervision and central resources is much higher than we expected.

We have to show that in order to deliver quality work we have to have an infrastructure and support systems to support and direct that work. We have had to satisfy ourselves that our indirect costs are reasonable and fair – and not pulling money away from services. After years of being willing to 'do it on the cheap', we have a job of work to do with our main funders and commissioners to explain to them the real cost of operating.

Finance officer, rural community agency

With regard to costs, I would be happy with a level playing field. At a recent contract review meeting, the statutory body sent along an Assistant Director, Commissioning Manager, Accountant, Contract Manager, Contract Officer and Finance Assistant to review a £34,000 contract. What are their overhead costs?

Treasurer, mental health charity

Costs: the reality

'Forty-three per cent of charities delivering public services say they are not achieving full cost recovery. And this doesn't, unfortunately, mean that 57 per cent are. Around 38 per cent say they only achieve full cost recovery some of the time and – slightly perplexingly – the remaining seven per cent don't know if they're achieving it or not.

'But the bottom line – and this is critical – is that only 12 per cent of charities delivering public services achieve full cost recovery all of the time.

'The implications for those not in this 12 per cent are serious. It is not clear from the responses to our survey why charities are undertaking service provision which they must subsidise from other income sources, or how they intend to make up the deficit. In some cases it seems that the charities themselves have no idea how they came to be in this position.

'Consistent under-funding cannot but threaten a charity's very existence. First, innovation and the development of new services are threatened. Then quality and effectiveness of the range of services offered is undermined. Finally, at worst, the funding dries up and the charity collapses.'

Dame Suzi Leather
Chair, The Charity Commission,
launching the Commission's report:
Stand and Deliver: The future of charities delivering public services, 2007

In full cost recovery a bid needs to cover all the direct costs and an agreed proportion of the support and organisational costs. The ACEVO/NPC approach sets out a template to divide up and allocate costs throughout an organisation.

The whole issue of full costing has proved to be a difficult and contentious one. In the past, some funding bodies have been reluctant to pay for what they see as management or bureaucratic costs and insist that their resources should only be spent on direct service delivery or have imposed an arbitrary fixed limit as to how much can be paid for overhead or core costs.

Management costs

In the past voluntary organisations have often tried to hide away their management costs. They have attempted to disguise management costs as service delivery costs or have even taken on a service in the full knowledge that their organisation would have to subsidise the cost of managing and supporting it. In the medium to longer term, hiding away management costs or reducing them to an absolute minimum is not a sustainable or viable strategy for any organisation.

Your bid should therefore be based on the following assumptions:

- That the organisation's management and infrastructure adds value to the service by providing sound management and business support. This support adds value to the service by making it efficient, ensuring that it complies with relevant laws and standards and providing necessary supervision and support to the service.
- That the indirect costs charged to the service have been arrived at on a fair and reasonable basis.
- That the indirect costs charged to the service represent good value for money.

Costs that are often neglected

According to an experienced voluntary sector finance manager there are six types of cost that often require special consideration when putting together bids.

Fixed costs and variable costs

Most activities are made up of fixed and variable costs. Fixed costs have to be covered regardless of how much or how often a service is used. Variable costs are incurred each time a service is used.

'A purchaser decided to move away from a block contract to deliver a training course for a particular client group to a spot or unit purchase. In the past the agency received a single service agreement to deliver a training programme for up to 16 clients. The purchaser decided to change to a spot purchase basis whereby each time a client was referred to us we received a fee. This caused us problems. Most of the costs involved in running the training course are fixed – venue costs, tutor fees and administration remain the same and have to be paid for if four students turn up or if 16 turn up. We had to work out a break-even point as to how many students did we need to cover the fixed costs. The transaction cost was also greater, as the contract for every individual student had to be processed and agreed and the fee for them invoiced. We managed to include an element in each unit contract price to cover our fixed costs when numbers were low.

Cash-flow costs

'Often public bodies insist on paying contract fees retrospectively – for example quarterly in arrears. Often grant aid was paid up front in advance. The purchaser might argue that you don't pay someone until they have started work. However, paying in arrears can cause us cash-flow problems. The cost of coping with cash-flow such as overdraft charges are a cost of the contract.

(continued)

Costs that are often neglected (continued)

Start-up costs

'Often in a new service an organisation will incur extra charges involved in setting the service up, opening it and launching it. In one case, it took a while for a service to be fully established, as referrals did not come through as quickly as we anticipated. In the first three months, we were faced with higher expenditure and lower income, as our client numbers were low.

Closure costs

'All the contracts that we have taken on have been for a fixed term. Some we have been able to extend or renew. However, in a few cases we have incurred extra costs involved in closing a service.

Goodwill costs

'Several of our projects are relatively cheap to operate because of people's goodwill towards us. One of our services operates out of a building owned by a local church. They only charge us a nominal peppercorn rent. We now carry out an exercise to cost this goodwill and make it clear to purchasers that the fee is dependent on this goodwill continuing.'

Two further issues need to be considered before costing the service you are bidding for; the issue of value added tax (VAT) and the costs involved in taking over an existing service.

VAT

Value added tax is a tax chargeable on the supply of services. In general terms, this occurs under a contract whereas a traditional grant-aid arrangement provides support to the organisation, not a service, so there is no 'supply of services' to be taxed.

Charities receive no special treatment in respect of VAT on their business activities. VAT registration is required if taxable turnover exceeds the statutory limit ($64,000 in January 2008, but subject to regular revision) If a voluntary organisation makes 'taxable business supplies' above the VAT registration threshold it must register for VAT in the same way as any other business. Failure to register for VAT as soon as required can lead to penalties being charged.

Taxable business supplies means turnover resulting from business activities that have a standard, reduced or zero VAT rating. Some business activities are exempt from VAT altogether so would not be included when working out whether you need to register for VAT.

It is important to take proper independent advice as to whether any of your organisation's activities could be regarded as a trading activity that could take it towards the VAT registration threshold. Once registered, an organisation has to add VAT to the price of a bid if the service would be regarded as a taxable supply.

Cost of transferring staff – the TUPE rules

The Transfer of Undertakings (Protection of Employment) Regulations 2006 (TUPE) protect the rights of employees who are transferred from one employer to another, requiring the old employer to inform and consult with staff who are affected and obliging the new employer to maintain certain terms and conditions such as pay, leave and pension entitlements. This could become relevant if your organisation is bidding to take over an existing service (or part of one) that is currently being provided by another organisation.

If a bid could involve taking over an existing service or activity it is important that a bidder decides if the TUPE regulations could apply. If so, the bidder needs to obtain from the commissioner precise details of the contractual and other details of staff that could be transferred over. The bidder will then need to include in its bid the cost of continuing with the terms and conditions of transferred staff.

Some commissioners include in their contracts a term that it is the responsibility of the provider to determine if TUPE might apply and also include a clause in contracts requiring that providers give information to other agencies about the costs and conditions of staff so that exiting agencies can cost and develop tenders.

Pricing the bid

Once the full cost of a service has been established, the next stage is to price the contract. Costing should be a logical process based on identifying the different elements involved in managing, supporting and delivering a service and pulling them together. Pricing, on the other hand, is more of a tactical and subjective process. It involves making judgements about how much the commissioner expects to pay, the price of possible alternatives and the state of the market. In broad terms, there are three main approaches to pricing:

- **At or plus cost**
  The bidder work outs the full cost of the service and then adds an element to allow for the risk of costs being wrong or to create a surplus to allow the organisation to invest in future activities.
- **Under cost**
  An agency is prepared to take on a contract in the full knowledge that the contract fee does not cover the full costs involved in managing and delivering it.
- **The market sets the price**
  In some circumstances, the commissioner will indicate in the specification a guide to how much it expects to pay. In some sectors there is a 'going rate', often established through custom and practice where existing providers have agreed a rate to be paid for a particular service. Where the price has already been set, you will need to do a full costing exercise to ensure that the proposed price covers your anticipated cost.

In setting the price, a number of factors need to be considered. Often bidders believe that a low-priced bid will do the organisation some longer-term good, creating a 'loss leader' whereby purchasers are hooked in and in future years will be willing to pay a higher fee for the same service. This can be a dangerous tactic. An under-costed price might serve to create an expectation in the minds of commissioners. It may become harder to raise the price subsequently.

There is also a range of policy issues about taking on work under cost. It will inevitably involve the organisation in having to subsidise the contract internally from other sources. Is this a proper use of a charity's resources? In the medium to longer term is an organisation that regularly takes on work below the cost going to be viable and sustainable?

In circumstances where the price is set by the commissioner an organisation needs to satisfy itself that the price is realistic.

Being invited to bid

Here are some ways of ensuring that your organisation is invited by commissioners to bid for contracts:

- **Get onto approved suppliers' lists**
  Many PSOs operate an approved list system whereby organisations have to pass a test to show that they have appropriate quality and management systems. Once on the approved list they will be invited to bid for contracts as and when they arise. Some PSOs open the list application process at set times; others are willing to accept applications to be on the list at any time. It is useful to approach relevant commissioners and find out how their approved list process works and take steps to get your organisation on it.

- **Make a direct approach**
  A direct approach to commissioning managers can be a useful way of establishing contact and asking for your organisation to be circulated with details of future specifications.

- **Review published strategies and reports**
  Increasingly, PSOs have to develop and publish strategies and plans and also undergo external inspections such as 'Best Value' reports. Such strategies and inspection reports are usually public documents. Studying them can highlight weaknesses and gaps in current services and priorities for future development. This might provide an opening for your organisation to offer its services.

- **Put your name on email circulation lists**
  Several local authorities have developed email circulation lists where details of all bids are circulated to organisations that have expressed an interest.

- **Share successful work**
  A useful approach is to circulate evaluation reports, independent reviews and positive press coverage to potential commissioners.

- **Market your organisation**
  A proactive marketing approach can be helpful to establish your organisation as a potential provider. Circulation of annual reports, personal invitations to visit projects and attendance at relevant events can all help to raise your organisation's profile with commissioners.

- **Watch out for advertisements**

Writing the bid document

The following points are based on the experience offered by successful and unsuccessful bid writers and comments from commissioners.

- **'Follow any prescribed format.'**
  This may seem obvious, but it is important to ensure that your bid follows the format set by the commissioner. Under most procurement codes, tenders that fail to supply required information in the set format can be rejected.

- **'Use a positive style and active tone.'**
  Often bids are written in a dry and passive tone. One local authority manager described a tender she received from a community project as 'incredibly dull, worthy and uninspiring. I know that the organisation is actually very creative and dynamic, but the bid did not reflect the organisation's commitment and vision.' Use a tone that is realistic and confident, demonstrate past success and show that the organisation has a genuine empathy for the work.

- **'Show that you want to do this service.'**
  It is useful to show that the work fits with your organisation's vision and future strategy and how it complements other activities and services. To show that your bid is rooted in your organisation's experience and fits its strategic development plans is a much stronger message than that your organisation is bidding because it desperately needs the work.
- **'Show that you will treat this service as unique.'**
  Although the service might be informed by past experience and build on previous work, the bid should show that you have thought about what is needed and what is possible in a fresh way rather than just repeating what you have done in the past.
- **'Don't use jargon ... unless they do ...'**
  All organisations and sectors have their own internal language. It is sensible to check that there is a shared understanding about what key words mean.
- **'Show that you understand the issues.'**
  The bid should show that you appreciate what the commissioner needs or wants to achieve. It is useful to explore what is driving the bid and briefly refer to identified needs, policy directions or service strategies to show that you appreciate the context in which the service is operating.
- **'Avoid cut and paste bids.'**
  It is very tempting to base bids on previous ones and keep a file on a computer to which new bids can be simply added in. Although this can save time, it can lead to errors in your bids and also mean that all bids from your organisation appear identical. It is better to approach each bid as new piece of work.
- **'Have evidence available.'**
  A bidder should be able to back up and evidence any statement made in a bid document. A useful exercise is to go through the document and identify any claims, statements or assertions made and ensure that you can prove them by providing evidence if challenged in the bidding process.
- **'Do not assume prior knowledge.'**
  A useful rule is to bid as if you are new to the commissioner. Do not assume that because a commissioner has worked with you in the past that it has an up-to-date and comprehensive knowledge of your organisation's operation and systems.
- **'Focus on the user.'**
  The tender should be centred on the needs, issues and intended outcomes for the service user.
- **'Check that all requirements are fully covered.'**
  Ensure that your bid covers and complies with any specific requirements such as insurance, policy statements or specific procedures.
- **'Highlight benefits and gains.'**
  A common mistake in many bids is to include far too much detail about what you will do to deliver the service and ignore the intended outcomes that the service should deliver for the user. A useful starting point is to set out the outcomes that you expect the service to deliver or contribute to and then describe the kinds of activities and interventions (sometimes called the method statement) that you will employ to get to the outcomes.
- **'Stress added value.'**
  Listing potential added value features can give your bid an advantage. Bidders need to be clear as to what level of certainty they attach to the added value elements.
- **'Follow any marking system.'**
  It is useful to structure your bid around the criteria or marking system that commissioners will be using to evaluate bids. Make sure that all points are fully covered.

- **'Check any contractual issues.'**
  The specification or draft contract might outline or imply the kinds of contract terms to which the successful bidder will be expected to agree. It important to check that these terms are clear and are acceptable to you.
- **'Emphasise the capacity to deliver.'**
  The tender should emphasise that the bidder has the appropriate experience to manage the contract properly and deliver the service. Refer to similar experience of successfully managing other projects and evidence of sound and efficient management practice.
- **'Check your bid document.'**
  It is worthwhile getting someone to act as a critical friend and to proof read the document. As well as checking for grammatical or presentation errors he or she should also check that your bid reads well, covers all the relevant points and does not include any generalisations or untested statements.

Answering the 'So what…? question

Identify the key positive points in your bid and spell out the importance of each by answering the 'So what…? question:

Point	'So what?' answer
'We are a project run by and for the local community.'	'This means that we understand local community needs, get feedback on what works and have strong communication networks.'
'We have a strong management team skilled in human resources, project management and evaluation.'	'The services we manage get good management support – this makes them efficient and effective.'
'We have strong links into the industry.'	'This enables us to help trainees get placements and jobs.'

Bid presentations and interviews

Once the tender bid has been submitted commissioners may choose to invite all bidders or short-listed bidders to give a presentation or take part in an interview or meeting where questions will be asked about their bids.

It is useful to clarify what commissioners expect from the meeting. What format do they want – is it more like an interview or will it be a formal presentation?

Preparation is obviously important. An established approach is to structure the pitch around five key sections:

- the outcomes
- the context
- your plans for delivery
- about your organisation
- about your experience.

Making a bid

	Questions to address	Key points
The outcomes	What do you see as being the intended outcomes? What could the service achieve for users?	Focus on the end – what would be a successful outcome? Show that you understand the issues facing the service user.
The context	What's driving the need for service?	Show that you understand what is driving the need to have the service and the broader needs of the commissioner. Link into local strategies, national directions and other initiatives.
Your plans for delivery	What would you offer to get to the outcomes? What would be different about the services that you offer?	Demonstrate that you have an approach that is tested and will deliver or contribute to the outcomes.
About your organisation	How would this service fit in with your organisation? What can your organisation offer to support and manage the service?	Show that the organisation is established and that the service would fit with the organisation's purpose and style. Spell out the organisation's ability to manage the service in an effective and efficient way and emphasise that the organisation's core infrastructure will add value to the service.
About your experience	What evidence is there that the organisation has the skills, experience and competence to deliver and manage the service?	Highlight the following: low and managed risk sound track record the organisation has the systems, experience and people to be a reliable provider.

It is important that the presentation leaves the commissioner's panel with a clear message: that the bidder understands what is needed and wanted, has thought through how best to deliver this and has the organisational and management capacity to support and deliver the service.

Making a bid

CASE STUDY: Make your presentation come alive

A commissioning manager described her recent experience of receiving two different sorts of presentations.

'We decided to invite two organisations in to make a presentation about their bid for a service contract. The first organisation was an established organisation, which had obviously put a lot of work into designing their presentation. They started off by giving us a 10 minute PowerPoint presentation about their organisation. It was a very slick and polished presentation. It seemed to go on for ages about their history, rate of organisational growth, management structure and operational policies. The presentation left very little space or time for questions, which was just as well as the four managers they sent in were not directly involved in client services – they were about business development and marketing. At the end of their presentation the only thing that I had learnt was that they were good at designing PowerPoint presentations.

'The next presentation was from a much smaller and recently established organisation. The two people they sent did a very short introduction and then managed to get a conversation going between them and us. They related everything to their experience of the client group. Through case studies and because both of them were either directly involved in supervising or delivering services they were able to make things like quality standards and service models come alive. Although smaller and newer they felt much more credible.'

Situations to avoid

Some common errors in tender presentations include:

- Losing your key points by mixing them in with too many others – aim for three to five key points that the panel will remember.
- The media taking over from the message – audio visual aids and tools like PowerPoint are valuable, but badly used can detract from the message.
- Underselling the benefits – highlight what the service will achieve in the user's language. 'Enabling a person to live independently on their terms' is a stronger message than 'We will deliver a client-centred domiciliary home care service'.
- Talking too much – leave space for questions and comments.
- Not being able to back claims up – have an evidence file of case studies, examples, references and background information to back up any claims or statements that are made.
- Failing to engage – see the presentation as an opportunity for a conversation rather than a one-way pitch. Try to engage the panel early on by asking questions and sharing experience.

Making your case

	Issues	Making the case	Evidence to refer to
Price	Based on full cost recovery. Does it provide value for money?	• Need to show that the contract has been costed in a logical and accepted way to show the full cost. • As well as providing value for money we can **add value by...** • How do our costs compare with other providers?	Able to show that costs have been arrived at in a logical way. Need to show that the indirect and organisational support costs are reasonable and provide good management support to services. Collect evidence of added value.
Quality	Delivering outcomes. Service models have clear and documented standards. Meets users' needs. Achieves outcome.	• We can show how the services we intend to deliver are likely to create the intended outcomes. • We have systems and processes to ensure that users are actively involved in the organisation. • Refer to evidence or findings from any independent evaluations.	Evidence of quality through use of quality assurance standards. Documented good practice to ensure consistency. Past evaluation reports, users' surveys, etc.
Reliability	Safe organisation. Low risk. Can deliver – has the capacity to meet the contract.	• Our organisation has developed the management systems and structures to ensure effective delivery. • We have identified the following risks and have taken the following actions to reduce them. • We have completed a benchmarking exercise to ensure that our internal processes are effective and compare well with other organisations'.	The business plan should show that the organisation has properly analysed its position, has a clear strategy and has the skills and organisation to achieve it. Experience of successfully running other contracts should show that the organisation has a 'track record'. A risk analysis should show that the organisation is aware of risks and is comfortable in taking on an appropriate level of risk. The background experience of key managers and trustees should demonstrate a level of management competence. Good systems and procedures and evidence of good organisational practice should show that the organisation is capable of delivering the contract.

CASE STUDY

Beware complacency

Returning from holiday Sara was alarmed to open an email informing her that the outreach project her organisation had successfully run for the past three years was to be advertised on an open tender basis. It was only three months before the current contract ended; Sara had assumed that after a review it would probably be renewed. However, a recently appointed commissioning manager seemed keen to assert himself and review all existing provision in a contestability exercise.

Sara believed that her organisation would be stronger than other bidders. After all it knew the realities of running the service and had a detailed knowledge of the client group, what did and did not work. Sara set about drafting a bid that stressed the organisation's experience and understanding. It explained how the organisation could bring continuity and stability to the service. She wanted to show that her organisation was realistic and was a 'safe pair of hands'.

A few weeks later Sara was informed that the commissioner had decided to award the contract to another agency. At a feedback meeting the contracts manager explained to Sara that the commissioners were attracted to the successful bidder because its tender came across as creative and offered an innovative approach.

Sara reflected that her organisation's bid came across as defensive. It lacked any new thinking. There had been a level of complacency in the organisation around the bid. Three years ago the process of producing the original bid had been a very creative and challenging one. This time it had felt like a chore.

Your bid checklist

1. Does the bid cover all the requirements stipulated in the specification?
2. Might the bid involve existing staff being transferred? Have the potential costs and issues of complying with the TUPE regulations been considered?
3. Does the bid need to include VAT?
4. Does the bid include a fair and reasonable contribution to the organisation's indirect costs?
5. Does the bid highlight the organisation's experience and track record?
6. Does the bid relate to the criteria or marking system that the commissioner intends to use?
7. Does the bid show that the bidder understands the issues facing the client group?
8. Are the contractual terms and expectations stated or implied in the specification satisfactory?

9   Is all supporting information (e.g. accounts, business plan) requested by the commissioner attached to the bid?
10 Can all claims and selling points be backed up with evidence or real examples?
11 Is the bid submitted in line with the requirements outlined in the invitation to tender?

CASE STUDY

Have we made the right decision?

'We have been running an advocacy service since 1998 for a neighbouring primary care trust (PCT). They had approached us to set up and run the service because we had a good reputation in the field and they had no local organisation to do it. We invested a lot of time and effort and developed a good reliable service.

'Last year the PCT decided to put it out to tender. They had a new commissioning framework involving three different bodies, with different commissioning officers for each one. They rewrote the specification putting in extra work and reducing the value of the tender by £8,000. We had to complete an organisational questionnaire and write our own proposal based on the price and spec. We were invited, along with three other organisations, to make a presentation. In addition to the commissioning officers there was a service user on the panel. We did not know the criteria for the assessment beforehand. We did win the tender but going through the tendering process involved an enormous amount of work for the organisation and I am not sure if it was worth it. Implementing the contract has been difficult and the monitoring arrangements are not clear. I was called in for a contract monitoring meeting last week at a day's notice and with no agenda. After the meeting I felt as if I had been in the headmaster's study!

'I am not sure if the organisation will tender again for the service. There was a feeling of having a moral obligation to staff and to existing service users and I do think our passion for the area of work got in the way of making an objective decision about whether tendering for the contract was in the best interests of the wider organisation. I think it is very hard to build up effective working relationships in a competitive environment, particularly when there is no history and you are not involved in local networks.'

Manager, local mental health charity

6 Agreeing a contract

Whilst contracts vary in format and style, most will include the following headings.

Contract heading	Main content
Parties	Whom the contract is between.
Recitals/Background	Explanatory information which is not legally binding.
Definitions	The meaning given to terms used in the contract.
Purpose of the agreement	An outline statement of what the agreement is intended to do.
Duration of the agreement/Term	The length of the contract.
Description of the client group	Who the service is for and how clients access the service.
Services specification	Description of services to be provided (often outlined in a service specification as an appendix to the contract).
Monitoring and evaluation	An outline of how the contract will be monitored and the performance data that the provider is required to supply.
Quality standards/systems	An outline of what standards should apply to ensure quality of service.
Costs, fees and payments	This should include the fee to be paid and the basis for it, a mechanism for upgrading the fee (where applicable) and the payment schedule. It should also state whether VAT is included or excluded. If the agreement is silent, VAT will be deemed to be included within the stated price and cannot be charged on top.
Management arrangements	Outline of who is responsible for managing the relationship and any areas of joint responsibility.
Dispute resolution procedure	The way in which any disagreement between the purchaser and provider relating to the contract is resolved.
Termination	The circumstances in which the contract can be ended, often with additional information about what obligations exist or continue once the contract is ended.
Non-compliance	A clause outlining what actions the purchaser will take if it does not feel the terms of the contract are being met. This should be aligned to the disputes procedure.
Variations	A description of how to amend, vary or terminate the agreement.
Limitation of liability	Where one or more of the parties try to limit how much they would have to pay if the contract is broken or something goes wrong.
Assignment and sub-contracting	This permits or limits the provider's ability to transfer the contract or parts of the contract elsewhere.
Insurance and indemnity	Specific requirements to have insurance or to indemnify the purchaser.
Agreement	The signatures of responsible officers.

Model agreements

More and more purchasers are moving towards having a model agreement with successful bidders; this is sent out to all prospective bidders with the tendering pack. In most cases a bid is made on the basis of the terms outlined in the model contract, so organisations need to ensure that they can fulfil any such terms before submitting a bid.

Some model agreements are quite prescriptive with very little within the agreement open to negotiation. Others offer a framework of standard terms but do allow for discussion/ negotiation around the detail. In some areas, local authorities are developing a 'two-tier' system, with simpler contract agreements being offered for lower-cost bids and a more complex agreement for larger contracts.

Avoiding common problems

Many local authorities have struggled with developing contracts for services that have historically been provided by the voluntary sector. This is partly due to the traditional relationship between the sectors of benevolent funder/grateful recipient and partly due to the emergence of service level agreements which (whilst attempting to put the relationship onto a more business-like footing and focus resources on local priorities) often failed to do so. In part, this is because most of these contractual agreements were simply designed to take over existing grant-aid funding and partly because the terms of the agreements were rarely enforced.

The cultural change involved in contracting on a competitive basis is one of the hardest challenges that local authorities and local voluntary organisations have to face. Yet without this cultural shift, contracts that are being developed contain fundamental flaws.

A useful check is to ask if a particular clause or term would be included if the organisation being contracted with was a private organisation as opposed to a charity or voluntary organisation.

Examples of problem areas include the following.

Funding and payments

Some contracts still refer to funding rather than the price of the contract.

Some agreements try to retain the ability to vary the payment on an annual basis, bringing in factors such as inflation and the commissioner's own available funding despite bidders being asked to quote figures for the whole contract.

A number of contracts refer to 'underspend' and retain the right to ask for it to be paid back regardless of whether the full service has been provided. It is hard to imagine a private service provider signing up to any such agreement. One local authority was considering including in its contract a clause on 'efficiency savings' which required the provider to discuss with the council the scope for savings within the lifetime of the contract.

Monitoring and review

Some contracts, under the guise of monitoring, ask for more information than is required to monitor the actual service. Organisations should be wary of agreements which do not clearly specify what data is required and avoid signing up to general clauses which allow access to records and staff without identifying both the particulars and the purpose.

When a contract is being agreed, it is useful for negotiators to pose 'What if…?' questions to test out the mechanisms for tackling problems and identify potential areas of conflict.

Information and confidentiality

There have been problems in a number of areas where service providers have been asked to provide the personal details of service users. In some cases this may conflict with an organisation's own procedures relating to confidentiality. Where there is a legitimate need to collect this information, organisations will need to ensure that doing so does not breach their own policies and values, that, where required, client consent is obtained and data protection legislation is not breached.

Staffing

Some contracts have tried to specify how staff should be recruited and managed. Whilst service specifications may include the level of professional qualifications required where this is necessary to fulfil the terms of the contract, the recruitment and management of staff is the business of the provider.

In rare cases purchasers have inserted a clause giving them the power to require a service provider to remove a paid member of staff or volunteer from the provision of the service. This type of clause is highly undesirable. Unless carefully drafted, this could place a service provider in the position of having to make an unfair dismissal, which could lead to an employment tribunal claim against the provider.

Access

Some agreements include very general clauses about access both to buildings and records. Whilst statutory rights of access (e.g. inspection) should be made clear within the contract, other rights of access should be on a negotiated basis and given only where they are necessary to ensure the delivery of the service.

Policies and procedures

Some purchasers have tried to make it a contract term that providers adopt their policies and procedures in certain areas: examples include equal opportunities, complaints procedures, health and safety. Whilst it may be important to the delivery of the service that such policies are in place, it should be resisted if possible and certainly should never be agreed to unless the service provider has received all the policies which it is being asked to implement and is satisfied it can implement them. Otherwise, those providers contracting with a number of purchasers could find themselves signing up to different policies depending on who was paying for the service.

It is perfectly legitimate for purchasers to satisfy themselves that whatever policies and procedures are in place are sufficient to enable the service to be delivered to an appropriate standard and most purchasers will have in the contract references to legislation with which the contract must comply.

Termination of the contract

Termination of a contract can come about in a number of ways and appear under different headings within a contract. The following are examples:

- Either party giving an agreed period of notice of its intention to terminate the agreement or by both parties coming to a mutual agreement to terminate within a specified notice period.
- Where there is evidence of service users being at risk of abuse from the provider or any of its staff.
- If the provider, or anyone acting on its behalf, tries to bribe the purchaser or if the organisation is declared bankrupt or enters into a voluntary arrangement with a receiver.
- Where the terms of the contract are not being met. In some cases there may be a separate contract compliance clause outlining the process to be followed. Compliance clauses should not only outline what action the purchaser can take if there is a failure to meet the obligations of the agreement but also what the provider can do if the purchaser fails to meet its obligations.

Any contract compliance clause should be clearly related to the resolution of disputes procedure outlined in the contract.

Legal issues relating to tendering

Tendering exercises can be carried out in different ways and the legal arrangements that apply can depend entirely on the wording of the tender documents. It is perfectly possible for tender documents to be worded in such a way that, when someone puts in a bid, a contractual offer will have been made and if the bid is accepted a binding contract will have been created. If this is not understood by one or other of the parties this could lead to one party contracting on terms that it thought were still open to negotiation.

Some tendering packs contain model contracts and specifically prohibit bidders from inserting their own conditions. The terms of a contract must be reasonably clear; therefore an agreement to agree to something, or to negotiate it, is not usually binding. However, sometimes it is not possible to agree everything in advance and exact details of certain clauses within a contract may be negotiated after the contract has been awarded. In this circumstance it is vital to provide a mechanism for agreement and a fall-back position if there is a failure to agree.

In the course of contract negotiation both parties often make representations to each other about the services to be provided, not all of which will be incorporated into the terms of the contract. However, in some circumstances, if the representations can be proved to be false and a party can prove that it relied on the representation and suffered loss because of it, it can sue for misrepresentation.

Clauses within a contract that exclude liability for misrepresentation, on the basis that the written contract contains the only terms of the contract, have been upheld in court where the clause does not also attempt to exclude liability for fraudulent misrepresentation.

Before entering a contract consider...

There are certain issues that third sector organisations should satisfy themselves about before entering into a contract.

- First and foremost the services to be provided under the contract should fall within the objects of the charity as set out in its governing document.
- Any contracts committing your organisation to significant expenditure and/or significant provision of services, and all new types of contract, should be approved by trustees 'in principle' before any major steps are taken to negotiate the form of contract.
- The trustees should also determine who needs to approve and sign the final contract – will the contract need the approval of the full board of trustees or a sub-committee?
- If the charity is a limited company or has a separate trading arm make sure it is clear with whom the purchaser is dealing.
- If the charity is unincorporated then one or more individual trustees will be contracting with the other party.
- It may be necessary to seek legal advice before even considering bidding for a contract, particularly where the provider is operating in unfamiliar territory, the contract is of high value, VAT implications are unclear, or where you may be taking over staff from another organisation and TUPE applies (see page 43).
- If you enter a contract you may be open to being sued for breach of contract if you are not able to deliver. You need to think about how important the contract is to your organisation and recognise that failure to deliver may involve not only repaying the costs of the contract but also paying the additional costs of the retendering process to the commissioner. The costs to the reputation of an organisation are harder to quantify but could be significant.

Negotiating the agreement

Whilst many of the terms of an agreement may not be open to negotiation there will be others which are open to discussion. It may also be possible, at the stage where prospective bidders are invited to open meetings or asked to submit questions as part of the tendering process, to negotiate changes in the service specification or model agreement.

There are four elements to negotiation.

1. Negotiation aims to create the conditions for exchange and agreement.
2. Negotiation is a voluntary activity – no one can force people to negotiate. Both parties have to be willing to participate in a negotiation process.
3. Negotiation involves influence, persuasion and problem solving.
4. Negotiation is both a formal and an informal process.

There are essentially two types of negotiation, often characterised as win/win or win/lose.

A win/lose negotiation is often very competitive and is often employed in a 'one-off' situation where long-term relationships do not matter particularly. Negotiating the detail of a contract for services is usually something that involves a longer-term relationship and where both parties cooperate to ensure that the contract can deliver what it promises to the client/service user. Therefore a win/win negotiation, where both parties use that common interest to solve problems and reach a workable agreement, is preferable.

Stages of negotiation

Here are the four stages of negotiation:

1 Plan
Work out your objectives.
Agree your boundaries and mandate.
Research and think through the issues.

2 Prepare
Identify your opening position.
Identify areas of flexibility.
Spend time predicting the other person's case.
Organise your case – work out your strongest points and your weakest points.

3 Negotiate
Start with ideals.
Identify common agreement.
Explore and test out options.
Control pace and process.
Check agreement and first steps.

4 Follow up
Produce record.
Fast follow up.
Check implementation.

Use a copy of the following table to plan your position.

Agreeing a contract

| Ideal position |
| Best negotiated alternative |
| Variable |
| Worst negotiated alternative |
| Walk away point |

Walk away point

The walk away point is the point at which you can no longer negotiate because you have nothing left to negotiate about. Usually the walk away point will involve an issue of principle. One manager of a care agency stated:

If the purchaser had not agreed that the details they were requesting about clients could only be handed to them with the clients' consent, then we could not have put in a bid to run the service. We understood why they needed the information but the trustees were adamant that compromising on a value which was so important to our clients would harm the reputation of the agency to such an extent that we would rather forfeit the service.

Unblocking a negotiation

Where both parties enter a negotiation with a clear desire to overcome problems then most details can be sorted to their mutual satisfaction. The following tactics can help if the negotiation gets stuck.

- **Stand back**

  Stop the process. Use an adjournment. Don't allow the situation to escalate. Work out what is important.

  'I think that it would be useful if we could stop now and meet again over the next few days when we both will have had a chance to think about it.'

- **De-personalise**

  Ensure that it does not become a personal battle. Hard on the issue, soft on the people.

  'This is a major problem. It is going to cause me incredible problems. What can we do to resolve it?'

- **Explore their position**

  Put yourself in their position. How do they see it? What pressure are they under?

  'I can see how that might cause you a problem. What would need to happen to meet audit requirements?'

- **Look for signals**

  Listen for any clues.

  'When you said that the proposed schedule was "unacceptable", does that mean that an alternative schedule might be acceptable?'

- **Ask questions**

  Probe. Ask open questions. Test out ideas.

  'If we were to change it so that ... might that be possible?'

- **Record agreement so far**

  Build on progress so far. Note what you have agreed on so far.

  'As I see it we have agreed points 1, 2, 3, 5, 6, and 8. So its only points 4 and 7 that we still have to make progress on.'

- **Look for hidden agendas**

  Look for what is not being said. Try to identify what might be driving a problem.

  'Could you tell me a little about the background to the issue?'

- **Generate alternatives**

  Suggest options and different ways forward. Develop and test them out together.

  'I think that there are at least three possible ways of tackling that problem. Can we go through them together and consider the pros and cons?'

- **Involve others**

  Change or bring in other negotiators. Their fresh perspective might see a way forward.

  'I thought it would be useful to invite along our treasurer, as she has experience of dealing with this kind of issue.'

- **Ask for help**

  Ask for advice. See if other people can suggest an alternative.

  'Might it be possible for someone in the legal department to look at this and suggest a form of words that would be mutually acceptable?'

- **Explain your position**

  Ensure that the other party understands your position. Explain the background to it.

  'I need to explain how this would affect our cash-flow forecast. We don't have the reserves to fund the service whilst waiting for payment.'

- **Decide how far to go**

  Is this a fundamental issue? Are you prepared to walk away and call the whole thing off or is it necessary to get some sort of compromise?

  'I need to ensure that you understand that this is a critical issue. I could not recommend to our trustees that we proceed as the risks are too high.'

Agreeing a contract

Sample Contract
This is a sample contract based on two real examples. It is not an example of good practice, but is fairly typical of the kinds of contracts being used.

Sample contract

Purpose of the Contract
To provide support services to carers.

Date of Agreement: ……………………………………….*(date the Agreement was drawn up)*

Parties to the Agreement
Lead Commissioner: partner representative

Name: ………………………………………. Position: ……………………………………….

Service Provider: authorised representative

Name: ………………………………………. Position: ……………………………………….

Start date and duration
This Contract shall commence on 1 April 20___ and finish on 31 March 20___.

Service to be provided
The Service Provider shall provide the service as outlined in the service specification.

Management of the Contract
The Commissioner and the Service Provider shall nominate members of their staff who will be responsible for the managing and monitoring of this Contract. The initial nominated contacts are:

On behalf of the Commissioner: ……………………………………….

On behalf of the Service Provider: ……………………………………….

Prices and payment
Prices

Subject to the Commissioner being satisfied that the services purchased as part of this Contract are delivered by the Service Provider, the Commissioner will pay the following:

Year 1 £43,000

Prices do not include VAT. Where VAT is chargeable the Service Provider shall issue the Commissioner with a VAT invoice.

Payment

Subject to the full service being provided, quarterly payments, pro-rata to the annual price, shall be made by the Commissioner to the Service Provider on or around the first day of each quarter via BACS transfer on receipt of an invoice.

Should the payment not be received by the Service Provider within 28 days of the due date, the Service Provider shall be entitled to interest on any payment overdue at a rate per annum equivalent to two per cent above the Bank of England base rate on the date upon which such payment first became overdue.

(continued)

Sample contract (continued)

Charges to Service Users

Unless otherwise agreed, the Service Provider shall only charge Service Users for the service in accordance with the Commissioner's notified charging policy.

Information

The Service Provider shall maintain proper records for the services provided and these records shall be made available at the request of the Authorised Designated Representative at all reasonable times excepting confidential files and personal data relating to specific Service Users. The consent of the Service User(s) will be sought where required.

The Service Provider shall maintain and provide such annual financial accounts as required by company and charity law and the relevant statements of recommended practice. Such accounts must be capable of showing that the money paid by the Commissioner has been used for the purpose for which it was given.

Staffing

The Service Provider shall provide suitably skilled, trained and experienced paid staff and/or volunteers to provide the service, ensure that the recruitment and appointment of staff is carried out in a fair and equitable way and that relevant employment checks for those working with children and vulnerable adults are carried out.

The Service Provider shall comply with all relevant employment legislation.

Outcomes

The objective of the service is to achieve the following outcomes. Achievement will be assessed during monitoring and review of the service.

OUTCOME	MEASURE	INDICATOR
(Insert)	(Insert)	(Insert)

Quality assurance

The Service Provider will be working towards a quality assurance system that includes arrangements for the setting and monitoring of standards and for obtaining on a regular basis and acting upon Service Users' views of the service.

Complaints

The Service Provider shall have a written procedure for dealing with complaints about the service that will be made available to all Service Users receiving services under this Contract.

The procedure will refer to the right and method of access to the Commissioner's own complaints procedure at any time.

The Service Provider shall supply details of any complaint made about the service and the Service Provider's response to the Authorised Representative without prejudice to any right of confidentiality enjoyed by Service Users.

(continued)

Sample contract (continued)

Confidentiality
The Service Provider shall keep confidential all information that has been obtained in providing the service. Information concerning Service Users shall not be disclosed to third parties (excluding any professional agency involved in the Service Users' care arrangements or requirement to comply with child protection and vulnerable adults procedures) without their prior permission.

Law
The Service Provider shall comply with all statutory regulations and enactments relating to the provision of the service and shall comply with any relevant directives or regulations of the European Union which are for the time being in force in the United Kingdom.

Data protection
The Service Provider shall comply with the Data Protection Act 1998 and any other relevant regulations made under the Act.

Freedom of Information Act 2000
The information contained within this contract and any associated documentation is subject to the Act and may be subject to disclosure within the Act.

Equal opportunities
The Service Provider, in recruiting staff and volunteers and in providing the service, shall be committed to anti-discriminatory and anti-oppressive practices and policies and shall not discriminate on the grounds of age, race, gender, marital status, religion, sexual orientation or disability.

Insurance
The Service Provider shall maintain with a reputable insurance company adequate insurances to cover such liabilities as may arise out of the performance of this Contract.

Health and safety
The Service Provider shall take every precaution to ensure the health, safety and wellbeing of Service Users and staff and comply with the provisions of the Health and Safety at Work Act 1974 and any other relevant health and safety regulations.

Sub-contracting
The Contract shall be carried out solely by the Service Provider unless the Commissioner otherwise agrees in writing.

Performance monitoring arrangements
To enable the service to be monitored and reviewed the Service Provider shall:
- submit monitoring data as specified by the Commissioner and laid out in the service specification
- participate in monitoring and review meetings arranged by the Commissioner

(continued)

Sample contract (continued)

Resolution of disputes

In the first instance the parties to this Contract will use their best endeavours to resolve by negotiation any dispute arising out of or relating to the agreement.

In the event that the dispute cannot be resolved, the Commissioner and the Service Provider agree to refer the dispute to an independent mediator to be agreed between the parties who shall recommend the terms of a settlement.

Termination of the Contract

Either party may terminate this Contract by giving no less than three months' written notice to the other. During the period of notice the parties shall cooperate to ensure that the interests of the Service Users are met.

The Commissioner may issue a written notice to the Service Provider if areas of the service do not comply with the requirements of this Contract. Such notice will require the Service Provider to improve the quality of the service in a specified manner, within a specified period. If an improvement has not been made within such period the Commissioner may terminate the Contract forthwith. Any dispute as to the appropriateness of the notice or sufficiency of the improvement actions will be resolved in accordance with the Resolution of Disputes clause.

Variations

The terms of this Contract may only be varied by agreement in writing and must be properly signed by duly authorised signatories of both parties.

Signed on behalf of the Service Provider

Name: ....

Position: ....

Dated: ....

Signed on behalf of the Commissioner

Name: ....

Position: ....

Dated: ....

Model contract

The following specimen service agreement is taken from *Jordans Charities Administration Service (Updating issue 15)*, Division L, and is reproduced by permission of Jordan Publishing Limited.

Specimen service agreement

Introduction

The specimen service agreement that follows is a very simple, short form of generic service agreement that can be used as a starting point for drafting agreements to provide many different kinds of service.

It is not recommended that you use the agreement without taking professional advice unless you are familiar with drafting and managing this kind of agreement.

Terms should be individually negotiated and not regarded as standard.

Probably the most important parts of the agreement are the service specification and the performance standards (schedules 1 and 2). These need to set out what the party providing the service will do, laws, where and when it will be done and to what standards. The more precisely these provisions are drafted, the more effective the document will be. We have of course, left the schedules blank […].

Agreement for the provision of services

Date: ……………………………………………………………………………..

Between:

Party 1 …………………………………………………………………………..

and

Party 2 …………………………………………………………………………..

1. BACKGROUND

The parties wish to enter into this agreement to regulate their respective obligations in relation to the Service.

2. DEFINITIONS

In this agreement the following words and phrases shall have the following meanings:

2.1 'Intellectual Property Rights' all patents, copyrights, design rights, trade marks, service marks, trade secrets, know-how and other intellectual property rights (whether registered or unregistered and all applications of the same

2.2 'Performance Standards' the standards to which the Service is to be provided as set out in Schedule 2

2.3 'Price' the sums payable to ………… in return for the Service as set out in clause 6

2.4 'Review Date' ………… and each anniversary of such date during this agreement

2.5 'Service' the service to be provided by [Party 1] as set out in the Service Specification

2.6 'Service Specification' the specification for the Service set out in Schedule 1

2.7 'Start Date' …………

(continued)

Specimen service agreement (continued)

3. PERIOD OF THE AGREEMENT

This agreement will start on the Start Date and shall continue for a period of ………… year(s) unless terminated earlier in accordance with clause 10. This agreement may be extended by written agreement between the parties.

4. OBLIGATIONS OF [PARTY 1]

In consideration of the Price, [Party 1] agrees with [Party 2] that it shall:

4.1 perform the Service with reasonable skill and care and in accordance with the Performance Standards;

4.2 maintain proper records relevant to the Service and will make these available for inspection by [Party 2] at all reasonable times on reasonable prior notice, and provide such other information as [Party 2] may reasonably require (subject to a reasonable charge should the information requested not be readily available as part of the normal record maintained by [Party 1];

4.3 keep in force a policy of insurance against third party liability limited to £………… per claim or series of claims arising out of any one event, and against employer's liability;

4.4 ensure that every person engaged by [Party 1] to provide the Service is properly trained and qualified for the task to be performed;

5. OBLIGATIONS OF [PARTY 1]

In consideration of the performance by [Party 1] of the Service, [Party 2] agrees with [Party 1] that it will:

5.1 ………… ;

5.2 ………… .

6. PRICE

[Party 2] shall pay the Price to [Party 1] as follows:

6.1 The Price for the first year of this agreement shall be £………… . The Price in each subsequent year shall be increased by applying to the Price for the previous year the percentage increase in the Retail Prices Index between the Start Date and the Review Date in the immediately previous year.

6.2 In addition to the Price [Party 2] shall pay value added tax at the prevailing rate, if applicable.

6.3 The Price shall be paid in advance by equal quarterly instalments on the following dates: ………… .

6.4 [Party 1] will render to [Party 2] a valid value added tax invoice (where applicable) for each instalment of the Price.

6.5 [Party 2] shall pay to [Party 1] interest at the rate of statutory interest as defined in the Late Payment of Commercial Debts (Interest) Act 1998 on any instalment of the Price which is unpaid for more than 28 days.

(continued)

Specimen service agreement (continued)

7. INTELLECTUAL PROPERTY RIGHTS

All Intellectual Property Rights used in or generated from or arising as a result of the work undertaken by [Party 1] for the purpose of this agreement shall (to the extent that they are not already vested in [Party 1] prior to their use) vest in and be the absolute property of [Party 1].

8. LIMITATION OF LIABILITY AND ENTIRE AGREEMENT

This agreement will start on the Start Date and shall continue for a period of .... year(s) unless terminated earlier in accordance with clause 10. This agreement may be extended by written agreement between the parties.

8.1 Except in respect of death or personal injury caused by the negligence of [Party 1] (for which no limitation applies) [Party 1] shall not be liable to [Party 2] for any loss of profit, loss of business, loss of revenue, loss of anticipated savings or loss of use or value or any indirect, special or consequential loss however arising by reason of:

  8.1.1 any representation (unless fraudulent), or

  8.1.2 any implied warranty, condition or other term, or

  8.1.3 any duty at common law or

  8.1.4 any express term of this agreement.

8.2 Except in the case of death or personal injury caused by the negligence of [Party 1] (for which no limitation applies) the entire liability of [Party 1] under or in connection with this agreement shall not exceed [the Price payable] (or which, but for early termination during such year would have been payable) under this agreement for the year in which a claim is made or (if a claim is made after termination of this agreement) for the last year of this agreement.

8.3 This agreement supersedes all prior representations, arrangements, understandings and agreements between the parties (whether written or oral) relating to the Service and sets out the complete and exclusive agreement and understanding between the parties relating to the Service.

8.4 Each party warrants to the other that it has not relied on any representation, arrangement, understanding or agreement (whether written or oral) not expressly set out in this agreement.

9. TERMINATION

9.1 Either party may terminate this agreement by giving to the other one month's written notice in the event that the receiving party:

  9.1.1 has committed a fundamental breach of this agreement; or

  9.1.2 is in breach and has failed to remedy such breach within [14] days of receipt of a notice from the notifying party requiring the breach to be remedied; or

  9.1.3 makes any arrangement or composition with its creditors, becomes insolvent, subject to receivership in respect of any assets or any administration order, or goes into liquidation or ceases or threatens to cease its business.

9.2 Any right to terminate is without prejudice to other rights in respect of the relevant breach and to rights which have accrued prior to termination.

(continued)

Specimen service agreement (continued)

10. CONFIDENTIALITY

The contents of this agreement and all information of each party relating to the Service shall not be disclosed to any third party other than to a party's professional advisers or as may be required by law or as may be agreed between the parties.

11. SUBCONTRACTING AND ASSIGNMENT

Neither party may assign the benefit or burden of the whole or any part of this agreement or subcontract any of its obligations without the prior written consent of the other.

12. FORCE MAJEURE

Neither party shall be liable to the other for any loss or damage, costs, expenses or other claims for compensation arising as a direct or indirect result of breach or non-performance of its obligations under this agreement due to any cause beyond that party's reasonable control including, without limitation, any act of God, war, military operations, riot, accident, failure or shortage of power supplies, abnormally inclement weather, fire, flood, hurricane, drought, explosion, lightning, strike, lock out, trade dispute, or labour disturbance.

13. DISPUTE RESOLUTION

13.1 In the event of any disagreement or dispute between the parties, the parties shall first endeavour to resolve it by referring it to .... and .... or, if they are unable to agree, by referring it to their immediate line managers.

13.2 If these persons are unable to reach agreement within two weeks of the dispute being referred to them, the parties shall seek to settle it by mediation in accordance with the Centre for Effective Dispute Resolution (CEDR) Model Mediation Procedure.

14. AMENDMENTS

No variation of or addition to or deletion from the provisions of this agreement shall be effective unless made in writing and signed by the parties.

15. GENERAL

15.1 Nothing in this agreement is intended to nor shall create any partnership, joint venture or agency, the parties being with respect to one another independent contractors.

15.2 Any notice to be served under this agreement shall be in writing and served upon the recipient at its address set out herein either by hand or by first class post or telex or facsimile and shall be deemed served 48 hours after posting if sent by post, on delivery if delivered by hand, on receipt of a correct transmission receipt if sent by fax.

(continued)

Specimen service agreement (continued)

15.3 Any illegality and/or unenforceability of any part of this agreement shall not affect the legality or enforceability of the balance of this agreement.

15.4 The waiver or forbearance or failure of a party in insisting in any one or more instances upon the performance of any provision of this agreement shall not be construed as a waiver or relinquishment of that party's rights to future performance of such provision and the other party's obligations in respect of such future performance shall continue in full force and effect.

15.5 This agreement shall be governed in all respects by English law and the parties hereby submit to the non exclusive jurisdiction of the Courts of England and Wales.

15.6 This agreement does not (and does not purport to) confer any rights on any person who is not a party to this agreement.

Signed by

……………………………………………………………………………………….. (print name)

for and on behalf of [Party 1]

……………………………………………………………………………………….. (Signature)

Signed by

……………………………………………………………………………………….. (print name)

for and on behalf of [Party 2]

……………………………………………………………………………………….. (Signature)

SCHEDULE 1

Service Specification

SCHEDULE 2

Performance Standards

7 Managing the contract

Once you have your contract agreed the relationship between your organisation and the purchaser will move into a different gear.

There are six key aspects of contract management:

- establishing clear management roles
- monitoring and measuring the performance of the contract
- dealing with problems and changes
- managing the end of the contract
- building the relationship
- the contract management relationship.

Types of contract relationship

It is interesting to examine the different kinds of contract management relationships that develop once a contract is up and running.

Based on our research we identified four types:

Master–sub-contractor
This is probably the easiest type to recognise. It is the same as any commercial relationship: the only concern of the purchaser is to ensure that the organisation providing the service does so in line with what is in the contract.

The emphasis is on delivering to target, contract compliance and doing things 'by the book'. Often the relationship between the parties is inflexible and slow to respond or adapt to changing circumstances.

Funder–supplicant
This relationship has carried over from days when statutory organisations gave grants to support 'good causes'. A manager of an advice centre describes it like this: 'when we moved from grant aid to contracts, I thought things would change and move onto a new way of operating. It feels as if we have the worst of both worlds. We have to write bids, produce quality standards, sign a contract and collect performance measures, but we are still treated as if the council is doing us a great favour and that we should be very grateful to them.'

Partnership
A partnership is based on mutual respect and recognition that both parties have something to add. Each party respects the needs of, and pressures placed on, the other. The aim is to work together, solve problems and achieve win/win solutions.

Collaboration
In a collaborative relationship both parties are working to a shared common goal. The focus is on achieving the results and respecting the different contributions each party makes.

It is possible to describe the management relationship between parties in a contract as a continuum between being close and distant.

In a close relationship there is considerable contact between the commissioner and the provider. Both the contract and the working relationship allow the PSO to be involved in or consulted over many service or operational decisions. There is also an expectation that there will be regular communication and reporting between the two parties.

The distant relationship is much more formal. There are clear lines between the roles of the commissioner and the provider. Communication is formal and based on formal monitoring and review systems.

> **CASE STUDY**
>
> ### Experiencing both ends of the close–distant continuum
>
> The director of a homelessness charity reports:
>
> 'With one local authority we had a contract manager who really was not much interested in what we were doing, provided our monthly reports were okay. All he was concerned about was that the paperwork was in order. He had very little knowledge about what he was purchasing. We had to work really hard to educate him about the client group and our service model.
>
> 'With another local authority we had a commissioner who liked to get involved in our day-to-day operations. She was forever "suggesting" what we could be doing, asking for reports and extra monitoring information and trying to influence how we managed. A colleague commented that if the local authority wanted that level of involvement then why didn't they just run the service themselves, rather than contract it out?'

Factors influencing the relationship

Several factors can create and influence the contract management relationship:

- **The agreement.** The contract itself will usually set out who is responsible for liaison and management.
- **Organisational culture.** Some organisations and some individual managers are particularly uncomfortable about risk. They generate controls, checks and balances to satisfy their need for control.
- **Reputation.** Past incidents and errors often result in the imposition of more controls and interference.

Either during the contract negotiation or in the early stages of the contract operation it is useful for the key parties on both sides to meet and discuss the following:

- **Mutual expectations.** How do both parties see their respective roles?
- **Type of relationship.** How should the contract management relationship work? What level of involvement will the purchaser have?
- **Risk and concerns.** What particular risks might cause most anxiety? How should potential problems be managed?
- **Boundaries.** Check that it is recognised that the provider is an independent agency that might play other roles.
- **Communication and reporting systems.** How should each party keep the other side informed?

Measuring the performance of the contract

The contract will usually state how its provisions are to be monitored, setting out the information that the provider needs to collect and pass onto the commissioner.

In developing effective monitoring and measurement systems two particular problems seen to occur regularly: over-measuring and measuring the measurable rather than the useful.

Over-measuring is spending too much time collecting information and data. Many organisations report that the amount of data they are being required to collect increases year on year. It is interesting to question how all this information gets used once it has been collected. One agency is considering having a performance measure to record how much staff time it spends on performance measurement!

Measuring the measurable is to focus on what is easy to measure rather than what is important (e.g. does it make a difference to the service user?).

The contract for an advice and information service listed a range of measures mainly focused on the amount of advice given. Measures included: how long it took to get through on the phone, age, gender and racial group of the client and numbers of clients attending outreach sessions. This was all reasonable information, but none of it reported on the quality and accuracy of the advice given, whether the advice was acted upon and whether the advice made a difference to the client's life.

The five elements of organisational measures

A well-established model for designing effective organisational measures is based on five elements: inputs, activity, outputs, outcomes and impact.

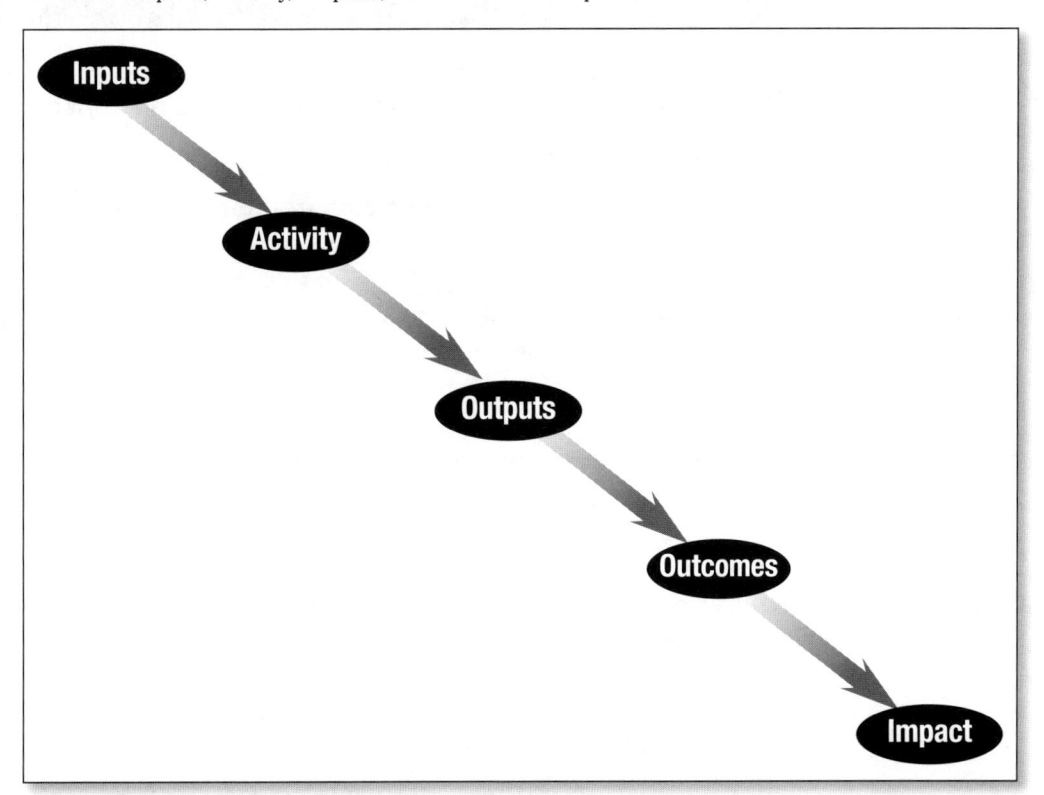

- **Inputs**
  The resources allocated and used to deliver the service. Examples might include funding, time and any other resource used to set up and deliver the service.
- **Activity**
  The services and activities offered. Some activities might be permanent, such as an information service; other activities might be one-off projects, such as running a time limited outreach campaign or a specific event such as a training course.

- **Outputs**
  The deliverables – what users get from the service. The outputs are usually easy to quantify. They represent what you produce or deliver. Examples could include the number of advice sessions, the amount of support provided and the number of training sessions delivered.
- **Outcomes**
  The differences, changes and benefits gained by the user as a result of the output. The outcomes are the changes that the outputs cause. It is possible to identify different kinds of outcomes. Some are about change – winning a case at a tribunal, helping a user to get something they want, changing behaviour or developing a new skill. Some outcomes are preventative – stopping something from happening such as acting to enable a user to carry on living independently. It is also possible to identify learning outcomes, such as finding out if a new approach works.
- **Impact**
  The impact is the longer-term effects of your work. Examples of impact changes could include policy and practice in other agencies or contributing to wider agendas such as improving the health of a community or strengthening the local economy.

Measuring outcomes

Collecting output measures has proved of limited use: often all the information reveals is how busy a service is rather than how effective it is. Increasingly, therefore, policymakers and commissioners are focusing much more on measuring the outcomes of a service.

Defining outcomes

Identifying, measuring and reporting on outcomes can be hard work. It is easier to quantify service outputs. For many people, arriving at a practical definition and working understanding of an outcome is difficult.

Some helpful definitions of outcomes include:

'Outcomes are all the changes and effects that happen as a result of services provided.'

The Big Lottery Fund

'Outcomes are all the changes, benefits, learning or other effects that happen as a result of your activities. Outcomes can be expected or unexpected, positive or negative.'

Charities Evaluation Services

'Outcomes are the "enduring changes" in conditions that are achieved as a result of efforts undertaken.'

A US grant-making foundation

Outcomes can happen at different levels; it is possible to identify outcomes from the same service for individual users, for groups, for services and for other stakeholders. For example, an advocacy service might create a range of outcomes:

- A user might get listened to for the first time.
- Gains won for one user might establish a precedent or change in practice that might benefit other users.
- Agencies might start a process of changing their procedures or working practice as a result of an effective piece of advocacy.
- Statutory agencies might also meet their policy objectives by funding an advocacy service.

Possible implications of measuring outcomes

The shift to measuring outcomes has a number of implications:

- **Outcomes need to be agreed**
  Sometimes conflicts and tensions can occur if people have different views or expectations as to what the outcomes should be. Ideally users, commissioners and your agency should have a similar view of the intended outcomes or at least recognition of overlapping outcomes.
- **The outcome may not be clear**
  Often we focus so much effort on managing the output that we overlook the outcomes. It is useful to start your planning work and also to start bids by highlighting the outcomes that can be expected.
- **Outcomes can be hard to quantify**
  Outputs are much easier to count, quantify and record as they are usually straightforward and unambiguous. Outcomes can be harder to quantify. Often measurement of an outcome requires a judgement e.g. 'Do I now feel more confident ...' rather than a simple tick box approach.
- **Lasting outcomes take time**
  Outcomes need to create some lasting change, which often takes time. Outcomes should not be 'quick fixes'.
- **Some outcomes are unplanned**
  Often some of the most significant outcomes are side effects or things that were not deliberately planned.

  Many organisations are still struggling to find simple and effective ways of measuring outcomes. The most common approach is known as the 'journey travelled'. This records where a client was when they first came into contact with the organisation and where they are now. The progress they have made is the journey travelled.

Designing and agreeing performance measures

In designing and agreeing contract performance measures it is useful to have a range. Some measures exist simply to show that the provider is doing what the contract requires of them. Others are designed to help inform future decisions about the service. These measures might be about picking up trends (e.g. 'more older men are using our drop-in centre.').

Approaches to monitoring

We have identified three ways in which contract monitoring takes place:

1 **Collecting and sending in performance data**
  On an agreed basis (usually monthly or quarterly) providers collect and submit reports setting out current performance. The reporting system is usually only quantitative. There is little room for interpreting or explaining performance trends.

2 **Holding planned review meetings**
  Some contracts have a process of planned review meetings. These meetings review current performance, identify progress and discuss future developments. The meetings can be a useful forum to influence future plans and future contract specifications. Some contracts allow for minor amendments or variations to the contract to be mutually agreed at these review meetings.

3 **Evaluating the service independently**
  In some contracts there is an agreement that there will be an independent evaluation of the service under contract. An evaluator is appointed to revisit the original need or purpose and see what progress has been made. The appointment of the evaluator and the agreement of his or her terms of reference should be agreed by both parties. The cost of the evaluation should be included as a direct cost of the contract. The timing of the evaluation can be significant: the evaluator must be able to gather evidence, draw up

a report and present it at a time when its findings can still influence future work. There is not much point in receiving an evaluation report three months after the contract has ended.

Useful guidelines

- **Look beyond accountability**
  It is often important to try to influence commissioners to look beyond accountability (is the contract delivering?) and start to share learning and experience. This can be about trying to move the discussion from 'what's happening' to 'what effect is this service having?' This might mean trying to focus on outcomes rather than outputs.
- **Use more than a tick box**
  There is growing recognition that quantitative data does not always give a full and rich picture. Not everything can be neatly reduced down to a statistic. Some things such as user views, feedback and satisfaction need a more open approach than the mere choice of tick box.
- **Identify added value or exceeding contract requirements**
  The service provider should also be able to use the monitoring process to identify and record added value and things it has done that have exceeded the requirements of the contract.

We are good at demonstrating how we deliver the service but not as good at demonstrating the quality of the service provided. We need to get better at showing how we consult and involve our users in ensuring that quality services are delivered.

Manager, local mental health charity

Dealing with problems and changes

Inevitably, problems and disputes will occur in any kind of relationship. Common sources of problems in the contract relationship include:

- **Changes in needs and expectations**
  What the users actually want and need is different from what was set out in the contract specification.
- **Unclear contract terms**
  There is confusion as to what the contract means.
- **Original idea or assumptions not valid**
  Things have changed from when the contract was originally put together.
- **Demand variables**
  The level of user demand for the service is greater or less than anticipated.
- **Cost variables**
  The actual cost of delivering the contract is significantly different from the agreed price.
- **Break points**
  Levels of demand are such that the service cannot keep taking on new work without reducing the quality of the service.

The contract should indicate how such problems will be tackled, especially if the negotiators originally posed some 'What if…' questions.

Effective contract management can resolve the impact of these issues by having an 'early warning system' to alert commissioners to potential problems before they become a crisis.

In building the relationship with commissioners a useful approach is to encourage the recognition of shared risk, to foster the idea that the performance of the contract is not just the responsibility of the provider. This can create and maintain an atmosphere of joint problem solving.

CASE STUDY

It just wasn't right...

The manager of a voluntary youth organisation was faced with a major problem. Eight months previously the organisation had been encouraged to bid to run an early intervention programme aimed at young people identified as being at risk of becoming persistent offenders. The programme would offer mentoring, practical support and training to young people.

A partnership group made up of local agencies designed the details of the programme. There was considerable interest in the project, including some national attention, as its approach was regarded as innovative.

Six months after its launch the manager realised that the programme was not working as had been intended despite the best endeavours of her staff team. The number of young people recruited onto the programme was below expectation. The time and cost involved in recruiting, training and supporting volunteer mentors was much greater than had been expected. Support from the agencies in the partnership group was starting to wither away.

After completing the second quarter's monitoring report the manager decided to take the initiative. She asked for a special meeting with the commissioners. At the meeting she described the problems the project had encountered and showed how the model her organisation was required to deliver under the contract did not fit the intended client group.

'At the end of my short presentation I could see that they were unsure how to react. I half expected them to see "poor performance" as a failing on our part. I knew that they would be concerned about having to report on poor results to their bosses. After some questions the mood of the meeting changed. The commissioning team leader shifted the focus from blame to what do we do now. It was agreed to redirect the programme and make it more flexible. We also agreed to write up a report setting out what we had learnt from the past six months.

'Looking back on it, I am really pleased that we took the initiative with the commissioners. I was tempted to hide some of the problems, just keep quiet and hope that no one noticed. However, we had managed to create an atmosphere that this was about shared risk and that the contract monitoring process was more about learning than simply crunching performance numbers.'

Designing processes to deal with problems

Processes need to be developed to deal with occasions when things go wrong in the delivery of the contract. This could include complaints about the service from users and operational problems in delivering the service.

Processes and procedures need to be designed that:
- focus on putting things right
- provide a fast remedy
- ensure a balanced and fair process.

Contract terms will usually describe how disputes between parties will be resolved. For example, a commissioner might be able to issue a 'non-compliance notice' if it feels that aspects of the contract are not being fully delivered. The notice sets out what action has to be taken to resolve the situation. Failure to resolve could lead to the suspension or termination of the contract.

Complaints from service users or other parties need careful consideration. Service providers should have the capacity to deal with complaints and investigate them fully. Commissioners should rarely get involved unless they feel they have a duty of care to the individual making the complaint or the issue is so serious that they have an obligation to oversee the complaint investigation.

Contract management needs to have systems and procedures that:

- are clear and understood (they should be agreed in advance)
- ensure that the service to the user is not unnecessarily affected
- avoid the escalation of a disagreement.

A disputes procedure is needed that focuses on resolving issues fairly (possibly through arbitration) and avoids the situation arising in which the contract is suspended or terminated by one party.

Building a relationship with the commissioner

The relationship between the commissioner and a voluntary organisation needs to evolve and develop. Organisations often put considerable effort into submitting and winning bids, but fail to manage this relationship once it is established. The following ideas are designed to create and sustain open and confident relationships with commissioners.

Involve them in plans for the future

Talk to commissioners about plans and ideas for future development at an early stage. Most PSOs operate to long lead-in times for a new development. One voluntary organisation found that commissioning managers often had a useful insight into future needs. 'We now meet with them around twice a year to use them as a sounding board for developing our business plan. We have found it a very useful way of getting a perspective into how things might change. It is also a good way of planting an idea.'

Understand their strategy and priorities

Time spent finding out the commissioner's future strategy and priorities can be valuable. Keeping in touch with national strategies and expectations, local plans and developments can be a way of spotting opportunities.

Ask for their feedback and advice

Often commissioners have an overview of how different services operate and the respective strengths of different agencies. This can give useful feedback. One organisation carried out a 360 degree stakeholder evaluation. Feedback from commissioning managers indicated that they felt the organisation had particular strengths and expertise that could be developed.

Develop useful measurement systems

Often performance measurement systems are lacking and amount to little more than number crunching exercises. It is frequently in the interests of the service provider to suggest the kind of information that should be collected to monitor the contract.

Take the initiative about communicating

One voluntary organisation commented: 'Every month we used to dutifully send off our monitoring report. After a while, I began to feel it was all going into a big black hole. No one ever referred to it or gave us any feedback. I now make a point of having meetings with our commissioners on a regular basis. A key part of these meetings is educating them about what it is they have purchased.'

Invite them to collaborate

Some organisations have found ways of involving commissioners at a professional level. Involving commissioning staff in events, training sessions and evaluation sessions might create better communication and understanding.

See them as an investor
A local authority senior manager explained: 'Often I feel some voluntary organisations only see me as a cheque-writing machine. The emerging commissioning relationship is about much more than funding organisations.' Seeing a commissioner as an investor is about creating a relationship that is focused on a shared commitment to making a real difference. It is about focusing on longer-term outcomes.

Develop a number of contacts
The trustee of a disabled people's centre commented:

Three years ago I would have said that we had a brilliant relationship with our local authority! The contract liaison officer we had was a real supporter of the centre. She took time to get to know us, regularly gave us advice and was very positive about our services. Two years ago she left and was replaced by a colleague who, despite being in the same section, had no knowledge of what we did. The previous liaison officer had not communicated anything about us back into the department. It was a personal relationship not an organisational one. We now ensure that we have several points of contact and have a profile within the department.

Avoid delivering sudden shocks
Bad news travels fast. A useful rule is to ensure that relevant commissioning managers are kept in touch and up to date with any developments or potential problems.

Celebrate and share success
A simple tactic is to make a point of identifying and communicating progress, outcomes and organisational success. As well as creating a positive atmosphere it can give commissioners 'good news stories' to use in their internal discussions.

Managing the end of the contract
The length of a contract can often be a difficult issue. Common forms are:

- **A fixed-term contract**
  The agreement will end on a set date, e.g. in three years' time.
- **A rolling contract**
  Each year the contract is extended or rolled forward for a further period, e.g. every year on a set date parties agree to extend it for a further three years.
- **A permanent contract with a break clause**
  The contract continues until one party gives notice that it wishes to withdraw from it.
- **A fixed-term contract with a renewal option**
  A fixed-term contract is agreed, but with an option whereby parties can agree to extend it.

Developing an exit strategy
Managing fixed-term work can be particularly challenging. One worker described a three-year contract as having a pattern:

We spent the first year setting it up [the three-year contract], trying to work out what the people who wrote the bid actually meant and what was needed. In the second year we developed some really good work and established relationships with other agencies. In the third year we spent most of the year being worried about what was going to happen next. Just at the point that the service was becoming successful and had an established reputation it was time to move on.

Managing the contract

Few services can be neatly switched off at the end of their fixed-term contract. The demand and need remains. Users and communities start to rely upon the service. It is therefore important to develop and work on an exit strategy throughout the life of a fixed-term contract to manage the impact of closure on all concerned. This exit strategy should set out a plan for either bringing the work to an orderly closure or finding ways of carrying the work on in another guise. Failure to manage the closure of a fixed-term service can lead to suddenly unsupported users, demoralised staff, lost skills and expertise. There will inevitably be damage to the morale and reputation of the organisation.

A useful approach is to involve the commissioner in discussing possible futures when the contract has ended. This discussion should start as early as possible, as it is important that the exit strategy is seen as a joint responsibility.

8 The organisational implications of contracts

Contracting between voluntary and public sector agencies is more than a business or a negotiating issue. It can raise many significant and fundamental issues about an organisation's role, independence and future. This chapter draws upon the experience of several voluntary organisations and looks at five key issues:

1 **The culture**
   The nature of the change needed to enable an organisation to be strong and independent in a contract arena.
2 **Sustainability**
   The need for an organisation to build a strong and flexible business model to avoid becoming entirely dependent on one or two main contracts.
3 **Independence**
   The need to ensure that an organisation retains and protects its independence.
4 **The role of the board**
   The need for the trustees or board of an organisation to become fully engaged in the contracting process and fully understand what the organisation is taking on.
5 **Organisational capacity**
   The need for an organisation to develop a range of skills, systems and processes to enable it successfully to bid for and manage contracts.

Strategic forward planning is required to deal with these needs; it is not enough for your organisation simply to be reactive. Management of a lot of these issues requires strong and consistent leadership from within the organisation, both to reassure staff, volunteers and users and to help them understand how the organisation can move forward.

The importance of organisational culture

Organisational writers describe culture as the 'glue' that holds an organisation together. It is a set of understandings, history and ways of operating that give an organisation an identity and ways of working. A manager described it as follows: 'There is a very strong sense amongst the staff and volunteers about how we do things here. It is not written down, but there is almost a set of unwritten rules about how we approach things.'

As we have seen above in other contexts, contracting can challenge an organisation's culture and ways of working. Some of the challenges may be gradual and absorbed over time. Others may involve a more direct change to an organisation's traditional ways of operating.

Our field visits for this book identified four regular cultural shifts made by organisations.

A change from funders to commissioners

As we have discussed above, in a traditional grant-aid scheme the relationship with public bodies was often a fairly passive one. The grant was *given* to support the organisation on the understanding it would do good work with it. The relationship with commissioners is usually much more deliberate and formal. Voluntary organisations need to put time into relationships with existing and potential commissioners to ensure that expectations are clear, roles are understood and there is a mutual respect between parties.

A perception of having to be more 'business-like'
Contracting usually increases the level of management tasks. Services have to be properly costed, bids written, performance measures monitored and costs and risks controlled. This can lead to your organisation having to invest more time and effort in an internal management system. It is ironic that at a time when some funders are resistant to the idea of paying any reasonable contribution to management costs, the management workload is increasing, often as a result of requests and demands from the same funders.

A change in the status of service users
Some commissioners are committed to involving service users actively in the commissioning process. Giving service users greater choice, developing better and faster mechanisms for users to feed back their views on the service provided and experiments in delegating purchasing decisions to users could change an organisation's relationship to its users. One manager described how: 'in the past we thought of clients as people with a problem for us to sort out. We now try to think of them as individual consumers with rights in the process.'

An emphasis on service delivery
Contracts are usually focused on the delivery of a service output or outcome. This can mean that your organisation has to develop systems and a management style that is much more performance driven. Your organisation now has to *show* that it has delivered the contract. In the past many voluntary organisations were more focused on the *process* of how they organised and managed.

In managing these cultural shifts it is important not to write off your organisation's past and imply that all that has happened in the past is now irrelevant or outdated. Contracting might require the organisation to be more accountable, more organised and more focused, but these requirements can best be built up from existing foundations rather than seen as an entirely new construction.

Three approaches seem relevant:
- **Focus on why**
  Taking on a contract should fit with your organisation's mission, values and strategy.
- **Be assertive**
  It is tempting to believe that all the power is in the hands of the commissioners. An alternative approach is to start the process by helping your organisation to be clear about its terms for entering contracting and recognising that, ultimately, the organisation is under no obligation to contract.
- **Recognise strengths**
  To contract from a position of strength your organisation needs to be able to recognise and show that it has proven expertise, a track record of successful work and the ability to tackle future work successfully. This can help your organisation to value itself internally and develop a strong culture.

Organisational sustainability

Contracting might require an organisation to go through a thorough reappraisal of how it generates income and funding. This is known as 'business modelling'.

A business model sets out the assumptions, relationships and processes that an organisation is built on. Voluntary organisations often move through several different business models as they develop.[9]

---

[9] Based on an idea developed by Bill Bruty.

Grant-led model

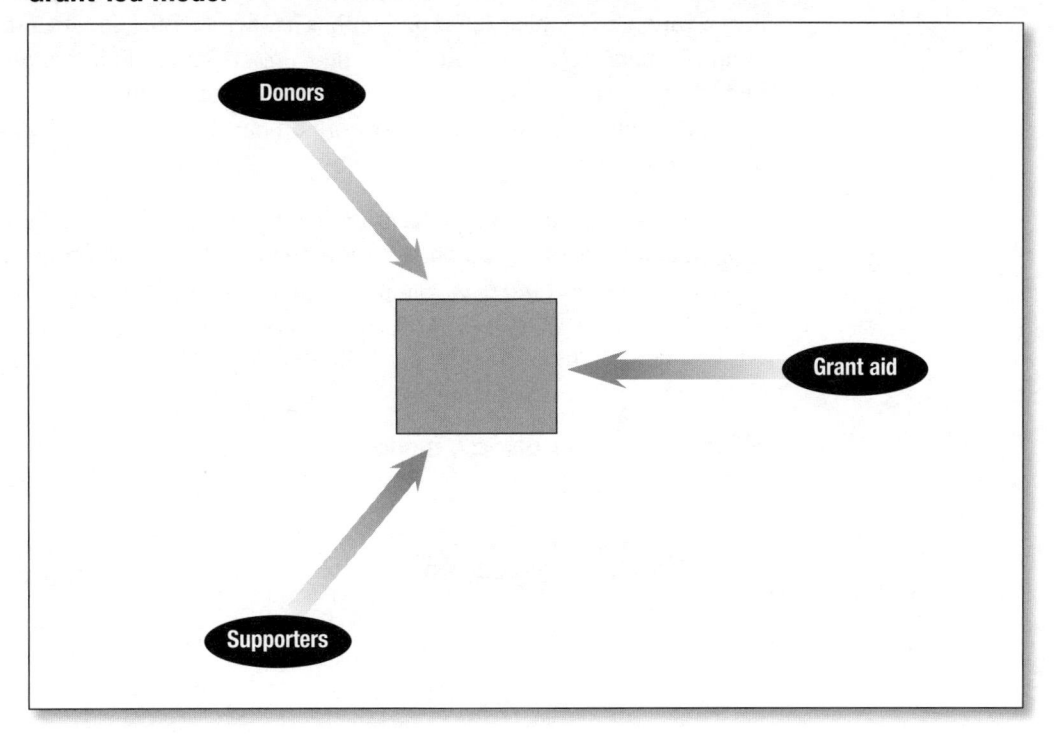

[Diagram: A central square with arrows pointing to it from three ovals labeled "Donors", "Grant aid", and "Supporters".]

The organisation operates by relying on the goodwill of a range of funders. One main funder often provides a major or significant element of its annual funding. The organisation draws in support from organisations and individual supporters who have 'bought into' the idea behind it. Often the model includes an element of 'in-kind support', for example, the organisation not being charged the full rate for office accommodation.

This model is common in the start-up phase or initial stage of an organisation's life when it is relatively uncomplicated. Managing this model is not particularly demanding. Key supporters have to be kept on board and in touch. There is some danger of relying too much on the continued support of one main funder.

Project-focused model

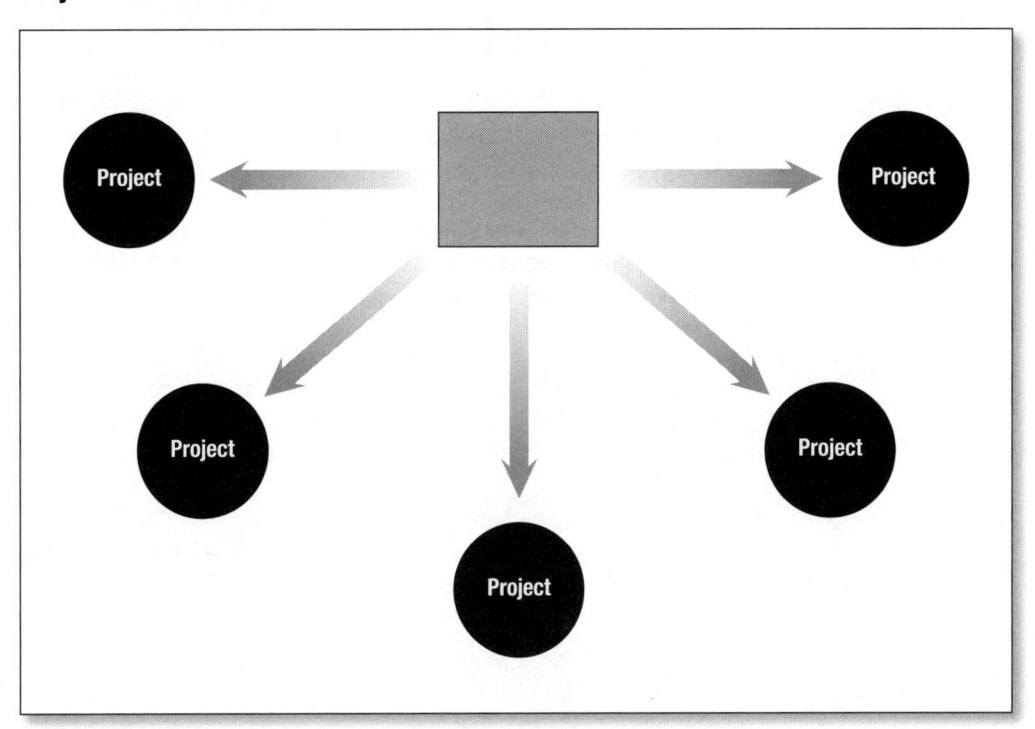

[Diagram: A central square with arrows pointing outward to five circles each labeled "Project".]

The project-focused organisation grows through taking on different projects and initiatives from a variety of sources. Each project has its own income stream. Funders and commissioners are concerned about 'their' project and not particularly concerned about the rest of the organisation. The organisation can start to feel as if it is a collection of projects as new staff are recruited to work on particular projects. Usually projects are for a fixed term.

This model does allow an organisation to grow and develop by adding on new projects. To operate it successfully an organisation needs a strong and flexible infrastructure to manage and support projects. Often the management workload increases in this model as organisations have to cope with an increased range of funders, all with different requirements. At the same time, some funders are reluctant to pay for management and support costs.

Mixed economy or diverse model

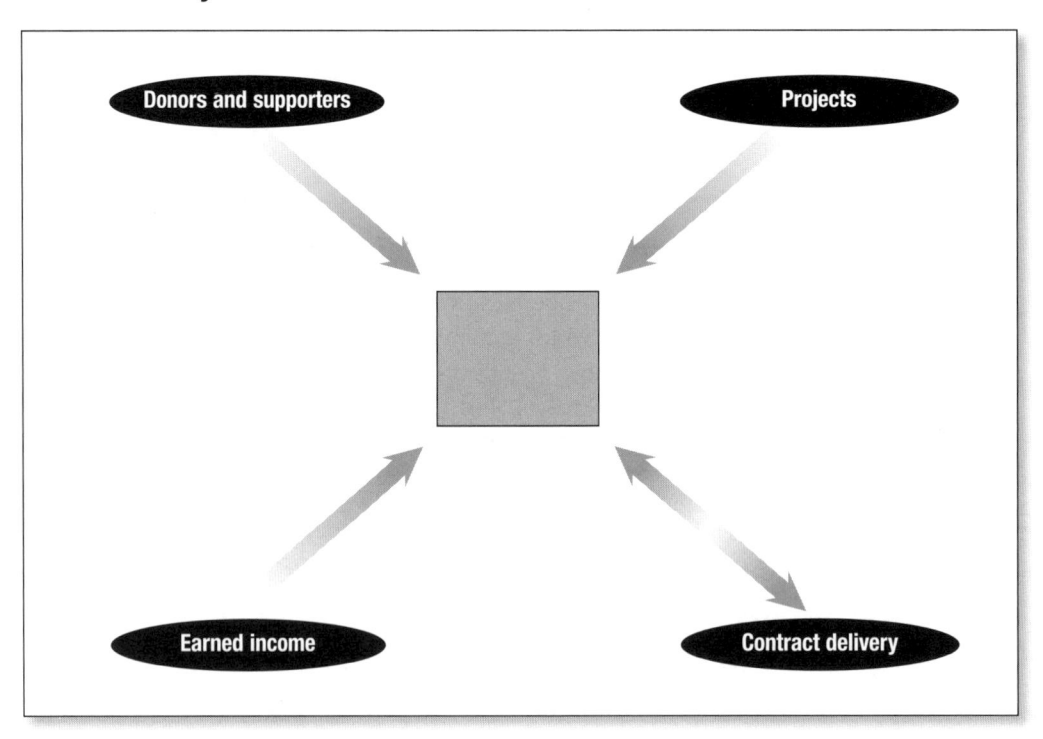

[Diagram: Four ovals labelled "Donors and supporters", "Projects", "Earned income", and "Contract delivery" with arrows pointing to a central square.]

The organisation operates to a diverse income base, made up of traditional sources of grant aid and support from donors, fees for the delivery of contracts and projects plus income from charging for some services and activities.

At the same time the organisation has to be able to operate as a 'good cause' to attract donors and grants, as a service provider delivering to specifications and as a social business running profit-making activities.

This model can give an organisation a level of independence. It is not reliant on any one single income stream. It might be able to use income generated from social businesses or charging to subsidise new activities or unpopular causes such as campaigning or piloting innovative services.

For this model to work a strong organisational core is required, capable of connecting all the activities and providing effective management and business support.

The organisational implications of contracts

CASE STUDY

Mixed economy model

The Tower Counselling Centre was established to provide support and help to individuals suffering crisis and stress. Over time the Centre has developed a business model designed to avoid it becoming over reliant on one or two main income streams.

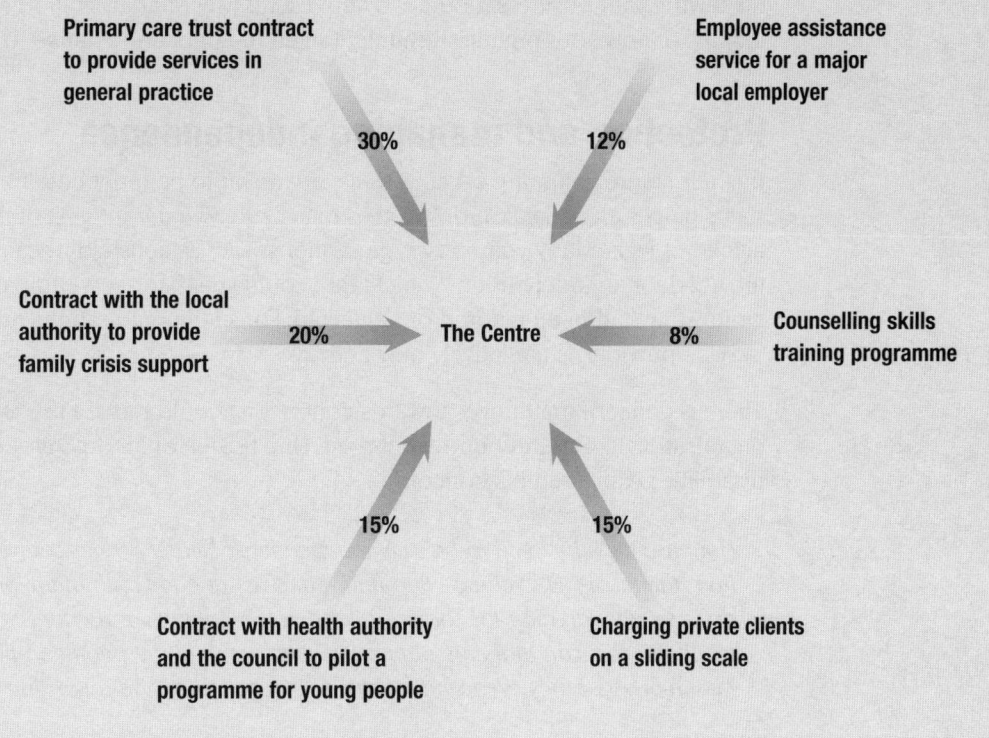

- Primary care trust contract to provide services in general practice — 30%
- Employee assistance service for a major local employer — 12%
- Contract with the local authority to provide family crisis support — 20%
- Counselling skills training programme — 8%
- Contract with health authority and the council to pilot a programme for young people — 15%
- Charging private clients on a sliding scale — 15%

The Centre's coordinator explains:

'The Centre's trustees felt strongly about the need to ensure that the Centre had a broad and diverse income base. Although contracts with the council and NHS make up 65 per cent of our income, it is a lot stronger than other local agencies that have "all their eggs in one basket". We insist that all services have to be fully costed and make a proper contribution to the Centre's management costs.

'The earned income – the work with a local employer, our skills training programme and our private client income – took a long time to get going. It gives us a level of independence. No single funder acts as if they own the organisation. We want to develop our non-statutory contract income sources. Soon, we expect to be able to use surplus from some of these activities to subsidise work with poorer clients.'

Five questions to ask about a business model

In most organisations the business model is rarely 'designed'. It evolves over time as circumstances develop. The following five points are useful in analysing a business model and helping to plan the next stage:

1 **Does it spread the risk?**
   How vulnerable could your organisation be to a slight change in any elements in the model?
2 **What drives it?**
   Is the model based on responding to a short or medium-term trend? Is it likely to last?
3 **What's the relationship between the elements?**
   How do the different elements relate to each other? Are there any examples of cross-subsidisation where one activity supports another activity?

4 **How are activities supported?**
   What sort of infrastructure is needed to sort and sustain the different activities?

5 **How might it evolve?**
   Which types of income are likely to increase or decrease? How might the model change in the future?

Reviewing your business model is a very useful way of analysing organisational risk and looking at how your organisation might need to adapt and change to remain viable.

Protecting and managing independence

By their nature voluntary organisations are meant to be independent bodies. Charitable status places an obligation on trustees to act solely in the interest of the charity and its agreed objects. Many voluntary organisations were established because their founders felt the need for an independent vehicle that could speak for and campaign on behalf of groups that had been ignored or neglected. For such organisations fulfilling the role of a 'service provider' is a relatively new activity.

There is concern that moves towards contracting could reduce the ability of a voluntary organisation to act, and be, independent. One trustee of an organisation for people with disabilities expressed his concern:

> *How are we supposed to be truly independent? Nearly 80 per cent of our income comes from the local NHS, yet we often find ourselves at odds with them. Much of the work we do is in campaigning for change, taking up complaints and criticising poor practice. Inevitably this can make us unpopular with some of the people in the statutory sector. I get worried if they are to be involved in negotiating and awarding our contracts.*

Protecting and managing independence is a core role for an organisation's trustees. It is important that all the different roles an organisation performs are given equal recognition. The management of service delivery operations is a tangible and practical activity. It is easy to manage and measure service outputs. However, other activities such as finding innovative solutions, working with users and influencing policy and practice also need deliberate management and time.

Some organisations have tried to tackle the issues of independence head on by developing codes of practice or, through the Compact (see page 26), maintaining recognition that a voluntary organisation is an independent agency and that campaigning and influencing is a legitimate and welcome function.

The director of a health charity described her experience:

> *We talked directly to senior people within the authority about our concerns. We got them to recognise that disagreements over policy and practice were bound to happen. They recognised that complaints are inevitable and indeed should be valued. They also recognised the different roles we had to play. We now include in all our contracts a statement of shared principles that recognises the need for user advocacy and encourages complaints and involvement in service development. It has helped us to have something to remind people that we are carrying out a useful role and not just being awkward!*

Independence can also be strengthened by ensuring that the organisation's business model is based on a diverse range of income and not upon one or two main contracts. Having some unrestricted funds, or access to funds not earmarked for a particular purpose, gives an organisation the capacity to take on non-service-delivery roles.

The role of the board of trustees

The governing body of an organisation – the trustees – are legally responsible for its management and direction. The way in which different boards carry out this role varies considerably. Some are very involved in the day-to-day operations of their organisation. Others confine themselves to taking an overview and delegating matters to staff. The move towards contracts brings into question the level of involvement that trustees should have in the running of their organisation.

The chair of a children's charity described the debate her organisation has had:

When our manager reported that we would have to bid for a service contract rather than a grant, we overreacted. Trustees asked that draft agreements would have to be agreed by the full board. Two of our trustees claimed business experience of contracts and asked that progress in the contract negotiations be reported on at monthly board meetings so that they could advise. The temptation was to get so involved in the mechanics and detail of the contract that we overlooked key questions like 'is this the kind of service we want to run?' We also tied our manager's hands by not being clear as to how much power she had in negotiations.

The following points are designed to help boards play a useful role in the contracting process:

1 Set boundaries
Trustees need to decide which aspects of the contract bidding process they need to be directly involved in and which aspects they could delegate to managers.

2 Ask 'what if...' questions
A useful process is to raise 'what if...' questions to encourage planning and future thinking. Examples include:

'What would happen if a service user had a complaint about our services? How would it be handled?'

'What would happen if levels of demand and take-up from users was significantly less or greater than anticipated in the service specification?'

'What if our actual costs were greater than anticipated in the bid?'

Such questions can start to test the contracting process and highlight potential problem areas.

3 Identify and discuss risk
Trustees should, on a regular basis, identify the types and levels of risk involved in any new venture. Trustees need to decide if the levels of possible risk are comfortable and if the actions being taken to prevent and reduce risk are robust enough.

4 Take the longer-term view
A key role for trustees is to safeguard the organisation's future wellbeing and ensure that it works towards its vision and values. Trustees need to make time to ensure that the pattern of services the organisation is operating is in line with its mission. In short, it is the trustees' role to steer the organisation.

Who sets the pace of contracting?

A trustee of a social care charity described the tensions that the demands of contracting caused in his organisation:

It all came to a head at our last awayday. Our director and newly appointed business manager gave a very up-tempo report about how the organisation had grown and increased 'market share'. They were keen to focus on areas of work that were likely to be commissioned in the future and move away from what they saw as unpopular causes. They presented an action plan of various activities they needed to carry out to ensure that the organisation was 'tender ready'. It was a very long list of things we needed to have: performance measures, quality standards and numerous operating procedures. Although it all made sense, it began to feel that the commissioning managers were directing our organisation.

After their presentation there was a very heated debate. Several of us were concerned that we were in danger of becoming 'just another provider'. Was there a danger of growing away from our user? One long-serving trustee commented that she had helped to set the organisation up because of dissatisfaction with the style and practice of the statutory sector. It now felt that all we were doing was becoming their sub-contractor.

Later in the day the discussion recovered. We started talking about 'contracting on our terms' and avoiding growth for the sake of it. One of the critical issues we as trustees need to protect is our independent identity and our ability to act and develop in the ways that we think are appropriate.

Organisational capacity

Many of the skills and processes needed in contracting are not particularly special or new, but your organisation may need to invest in or encourage particular skills and also develop some key processes to support its contracting activities. For some individuals this may mean a change of emphasis in the delivery of their role. A fundraiser reported how the move towards contracts and away from relying on grants led to changes in his role:

My role is now more about business development rather than a pure fundraising one. I work alongside managers to help them work with commissioners. We have found that commissioners prefer to talk to people involved in service delivery than to fundraisers. Now my role is much more integrated in the organisation. It is my job to spot opportunities, work with service managers to develop proposals and ensure that full bids go off in time. I am now more of a resource to the team, rather than the guy who gets the money for other people to spend!

Public service contracting can involve an increase in the transaction costs of delivering a service. Organisations have to put more time into researching, bidding for and managing contracts. Some of the organisational functions that are likely to increase include:

- **Marketing**
  Ensuring that potential commissioners are aware of the organisation's interests and expertise and that the organisation is invited to apply to be on approved supplier lists or to bid for specifications.
- **Costing work**
  Developing and implementing an approach to costing that ensures the full direct costs of a service are included in a bid, together with a contribution to the organisation's overhead and support costs.
- **Bid writing**
  Drafting and presenting bids in a way that answers all the specific requirements of the contract specification and also makes a convincing case for the organisation.
- **Contract negotiation**
  Having an awareness of the legal and managerial issues involved in putting an agreement together.
- **Performance measurement**
  Designing, collecting and analysing useful measures that show the provider is delivering the contract's outputs and working towards agreed outcomes.
- **Service evaluation**
  Gathering feedback from users and other stakeholders to determine effectiveness. Building up an evidence base to show that an organisation can deliver results.

- **Relationship management**
  Ensuring that commissioners are kept in touch once a contract is up and running.
- **Strategic and business planning**
  Enabling an organisation to focus on its purpose, think and plan ahead, clarify priorities and attract worthwhile investment in its service.

All these activities will take up organisational time. This could lead to an increase in the time an organisation has to spend on management and support functions rather than direct delivery.

> **CASE STUDY**
>
> ## Administrative break point...
>
> 'One key impact of moving into contracts has been a major increase in our management and administration costs. We are a relatively small organisation with seven staff and 30 volunteers. This year our organisation has 16 different income streams. Two service agreements with local authorities, six project contracts with various health commissioners, a lottery grant, a Learning and Skills Council contract and various other grants and supporter income. All of our public service commissioners require considerable management. They all want performance monitoring information, but in different formats. They regularly ask us for extra information to show that they are doing or commissioning something to meet their targets.
>
> 'The level of work that goes into bids has also increased. We have to do detailed costings and produce quality tenders.
>
> 'None of this work is particularly difficult, but as an organisation we have consistently under-resourced our management infrastructure. We have plenty of ideas about how we would like to develop, but I feel that we have hit break point.'
>
> *Finance manager,*
> *community health project*

Business planning issues

A business plan has two elements to it:

- an internal focus – to help the organisation agree priorities and develop a shared sense of direction and purpose
- an external focus – to explain to potential backers or commissioners the thinking behind the organisation.

It also shows that the organisation is clear about its purpose, is realistic and has fully thought through the implications of its plans.

From a contracting point of view, some of the key issues your business plan needs to include are as follows.

1 **The need to ensure a diverse spread of income**
   The plan needs to show that your organisation's business model is viable.

2 **The requirement to show that all costs are fully covered**
   The plan needs to show that your organisation has used a fair and logical approach to costing its services.

3 **How the management infrastructure supports the services**
   A key message should be that your organisation's infrastructure adds value to individual services by providing effective management and support.

4 **How the 'organisational fit' works**
   The plan needs to show how all of your organisation's projects and activities fit together. There should be a common thread between the organisation's different activities.

5 Managing risk

It is useful to include a simple risk analysis in the plan showing that your organisation has identified and is managing risk.

An established format for describing risk is shown below.

Risk	Assessment of likelihood	Preventative action	Contingency measures i.e. action prepared in case it does happen

6 Managing growth

Taking on contracts can often lead to organisational growth; your plan needs to show that your organisation has the skills and the structure to manage future growth and recognises how growth might change it.

7 Longer-term strategy and vision

The plan should explain your organisation's longer-term aspirations and vision.

9

Competition, cooperation and future possibilities

This chapter is concerned with some of the bigger issues surrounding contracting. It looks at three main issues.

- How voluntary organisations might fare in an increasingly competitive tendering atmosphere.
- Models and processes to encourage voluntary organisations to work together and cooperate.
- The need to ensure that an organisation retains and protects its independence.

Operating in a market atmosphere

In economic terms, a market is a place that enables buyers and sellers to meet, trade and exchange goods and services. Usually both parties go into a market expecting to become better off as a result of the transaction. The idea of a market in areas such as health and social care is a contentious one. However, it is useful to analyse the market in which a voluntary organisation operates and to look at how it might change.

Markets are made up of different elements:

- the level and type of demand for services
- the range and quality of supply available
- the type and shape of organisations working in the market
- the level of competition between providers
- how much purchasers are able or prepared to pay.

Increasingly commissioners are referring to the 'market' and also to their role as commissioners in managing and influencing the market. Often the market is ill defined or has structural problems within it. Problems include the following.

Market domination

The market might be dominated by one or two main organisations. They have a history of operating within the market, have a high degree of market share and have very strong relationships with key decision makers. One commissioning manager described how in his area:

> *We rely too much on two agencies to deliver practically all of our services for a particular client group. It's a very established and cosy relationship. I think both parties have become a little lazy. On our side, it's a lot less hassle to refer a client to them as opposed to chasing round looking for an alternative. Although they deliver a service I think that they have become complacent – they are not so good at dealing with clients with special or different needs. Although it is risky to rely so much on two providers, it is hard to persuade colleagues to look for alternatives.*

A provider-led market

Market provision and standards of best practice and quality have been defined by existing providers rather than users. Commissioners write contract specifications based on what has been provided in the past rather than what is needed now or in the future.

Lack of involvement of the service user

In a health or social care market the commissioner purchases services on the basis of what it thinks the user or client needs or wants. With rare exceptions, such as direct payments schemes for personal care, the user has little real or economic power in the market.

How to analyse your market

The idea of a market is still a new one for many in the public and voluntary sectors. Assumptions are often therefore made about how the market will operate. As the Audit Commission's 2007 report *Hearts and Minds: Commissioning from the voluntary sector* puts it:

> *In our fieldwork, we found that commissioners and providers had only limited understanding of the amount of competition in their service areas. In particular, we found there was an assumption that there is little competition for the largest or smallest contracts. At the high end, a few large suppliers will dominate the big block contracts; at the lower end of the scale, small voluntary organisations will dominate the provision of niche services because there is no interest from the private sector. However, there was a reluctance to test the market.*

The following points are useful starters in trying to understand the dynamics of your market:

What is the nature of your market?

- What is its current size and scope?
- What is its potential size and scope?
- How is it changing?
- How stable is it?

How does your market operate?

- Who makes purchasing decisions?
- Who controls purchasing in your market?
- How much seasonal variance is there?

What drives your market?

- Legal duty?
- Policy target?
- Aspiration?
- Need?

Who are the other players?

It is helpful to use the following table to examine who else is operating in your market and to compare the positive and negative factors of their presence.

Player	Positive factors	Negative factors	Key difference

- How do you differentiate yourself from other players in the market?
- What is your unique selling proposition (USP)?

What are the prerequisites for operating?
- Quality standards?
- Qualifications?
- Legal requirements?

Pricing
- How much do people expect to pay?
- How are prices set?
- Legal requirements?

The issue of competition

Competition between organisations is not a new concept for voluntary organisations.

A seasoned voluntary sector manager commented:

> *Our reaction to competition is odd. People think that our rivals might be nasty capitalists from cherry-picking private companies who believe that they can make a fast profit. It's more likely to be another voluntary agency from down the road. There has always been competition, we resisted sharing plans, made funding bids in isolation and were reluctant to genuinely work together. It was below the table and hidden competition.*

Organisations can compete on different factors:

- **Offering a lower price** – by reducing costs to a minimum or by entering a contract race with a 'loss leader' price a bidder might hope to gain an advantage.
- **Claiming better quality** – by arguing that the service model proposed is more likely to achieve lasting and quality outcomes.
- **Offering a reliable and established service** – by arguing that the organisation is a safe and trusted provider.
- **Claiming experience** – by suggesting that the organisation has a proven track record in delivering similar contracts.
- **Offering extras or added value** – by offering to exceed the precise demands on the specification and offer more.

Competition is often perceived as a destructive force. It can reduce a contracting process to a scramble over who can do it most cheaply, thereby reducing the quality and reliability of the service.

One experienced local authority purchasing manager commented:

> *I can think of a couple of occasions where we have evaluated tenders for work and been very concerned at the low price quoted. It led us to question if the organisations (in one case a private sector agency and in another a charity) had the infrastructure to properly deliver and back up a quality service.*
>
> *Our new approach is of using a 'two envelope' bidding process, where we first consider the bidder's approach to quality and the reliability of the organisation, shortlist only those that meet our standards and then go onto compare price. This has improved the process.*

Working together

Most people would support the idea of organisations working together. It seems illogical to have several organisations all struggling to do similar things. One strategic response is to explore ways in which voluntary organisations can work together.

The move towards working together in a contract culture can be driven by a range of approaches.

Cooperation not competition

Often the move towards cooperation is driven by recognition that three or four organisations bidding separately will inevitably put organisations against each other and create competition. Funding structures and ways of working together are an alternative to competition.

Working together to create better value

If organisations find ways of working together the sum of the parts might be greater than the whole. Organisations might be able to learn from each other, develop and share their specialisms and with time create a better service.

Avoiding organisational divisions

Many organisations develop and grow in an ad hoc way. There is little direct planning or coordination of effort. This often causes duplication of effort or an uncoordinated map of service provision. Working together might be able to create a more integrated and accessible service. Combining effort could also mean that bigger contracts could be won. In several instances, organisations have joined together in order to win larger contracts. Finally, working together could create 'strength in numbers'.

Working together in a contract environment

There are several different models and ways of working in a contracting environment. Possible models include:

A joint bid

Individual organisations decide to submit one joint bid, rather than each agency doing its own. If successful, one organisation might be appointed 'lead' or accountable body to manage on behalf of the others. The delivery of the work and the contract fee is shared out amongst the bidders.

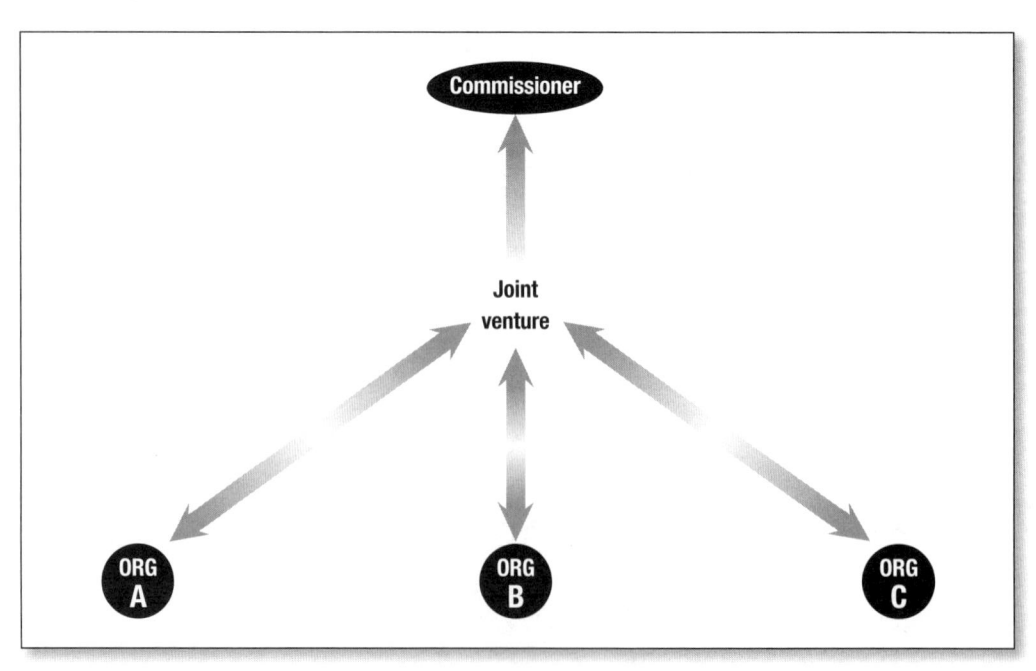

Potential advantages	Potential disadvantages
■ Organisations stay independent ■ Flexible structure	■ Depends upon a commitment to cooperation ■ Lines of accountability can be vague

Issues to address	Business questions
■ Role and powers of the lead body ■ Who has responsibility if things go wrong? ■ Need to identify and share each organisation's skills and expertise	■ Need to include the costs of the lead body ■ Need a fair process for sharing out work and resources

Creating a joint venture or consortia

In this model, individual organisations agree to create a new organisation to deliver a service. Usually the original organisations will stay involved in the new organisation and often exercise a controlling interest in it. The new venture will hold the contract, employ staff and manage the contract working alongside the original organisations.

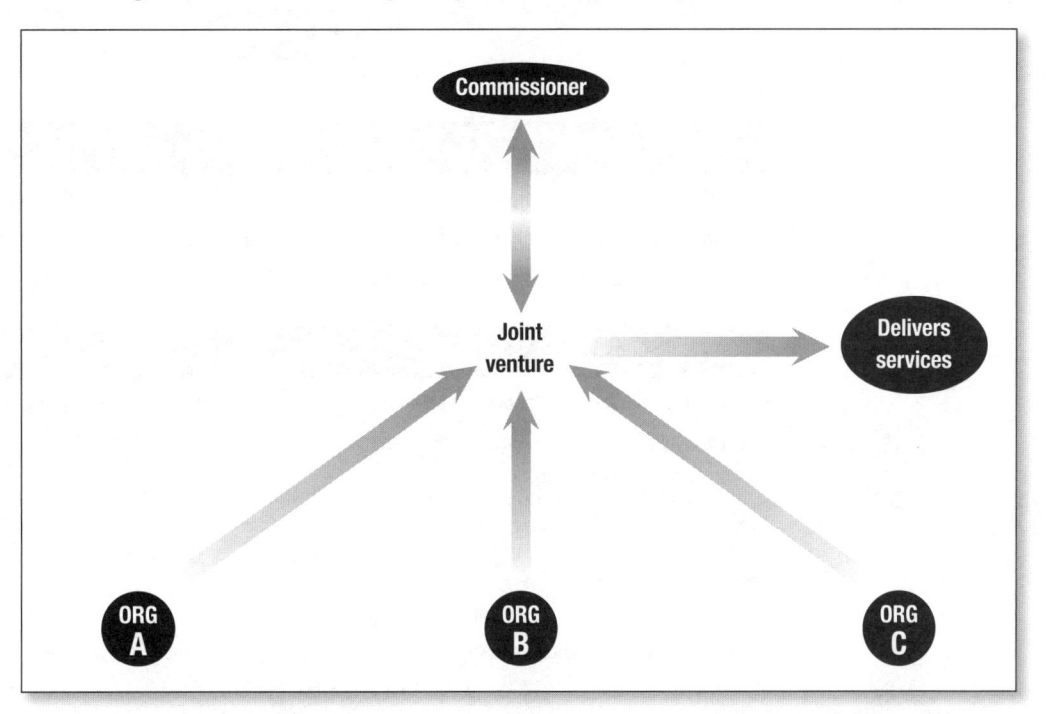

Potential advantages	Potential disadvantages
■ Can be a way of transferring risk to the new venture ■ Ringfences the contract activity	■ Can be time consuming and expensive to set up ■ Who controls it? ■ Risk of creating another organisation

Issues to address	Business questions
■ Joint venture needs tight scope ■ What happens if the joint venture company fails or underperforms?	■ Is it meant to be permanent? ■ How much does it cost to run?

Creating an alliance of providers

Independent organisations establish a formal or informal association to share information, lobby for better practice and influence commissioners. The alliance itself does not bid for or deliver contracts. It coordinates and represents the interests of independent agencies.

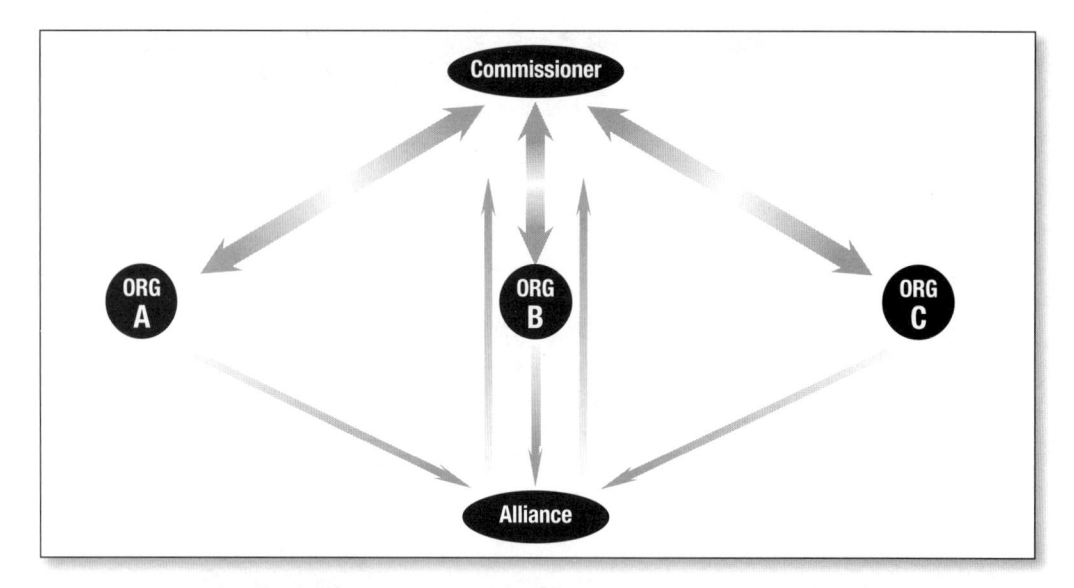

Potential advantages	Potential disadvantages
■ Informal way of encouraging cooperation ■ Not about creating another structure ■ Focuses on influencing and campaigning	■ Needs individuals committed to give time to lead it ■ Who pays for its running costs? ■ Who does it speak for?
Issues to address	**Business questions**
■ Often works best to a short-term agenda ■ Depends on sustaining organisations and individual commitment	■ Is it meant to be an established organisation or a 'virtual' organisation?

Joint service plan

Organisations remain independent and have separate contracts but agree to coordinate their activities. Working together might arise from the need for shared strategic planning and could even be a condition of the contract.

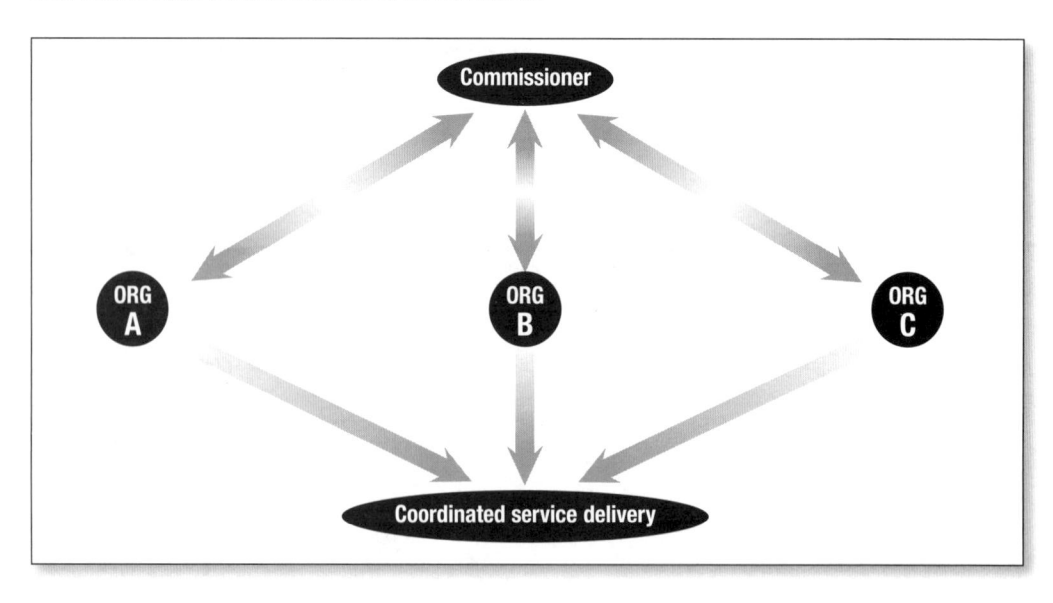

Competition, cooperation and future possibilities

Potential advantages	Potential disadvantages
■ An opportunity to take a big picture look at user needs, service gaps and duplication ■ Focused on the service rather than the structure	■ Relies on people being willing to work together. ■ What happens if organisations fail to cooperate?
Issues to address	**Business questions**
■ Start with joint strategic planning ■ Gives an opportunity for organisations to specialise	■ Need process and style to encourage joint working

Outsourcing

One organisation wins a contract but then outsources or sub-contracts an element of its delivery to another organisation.

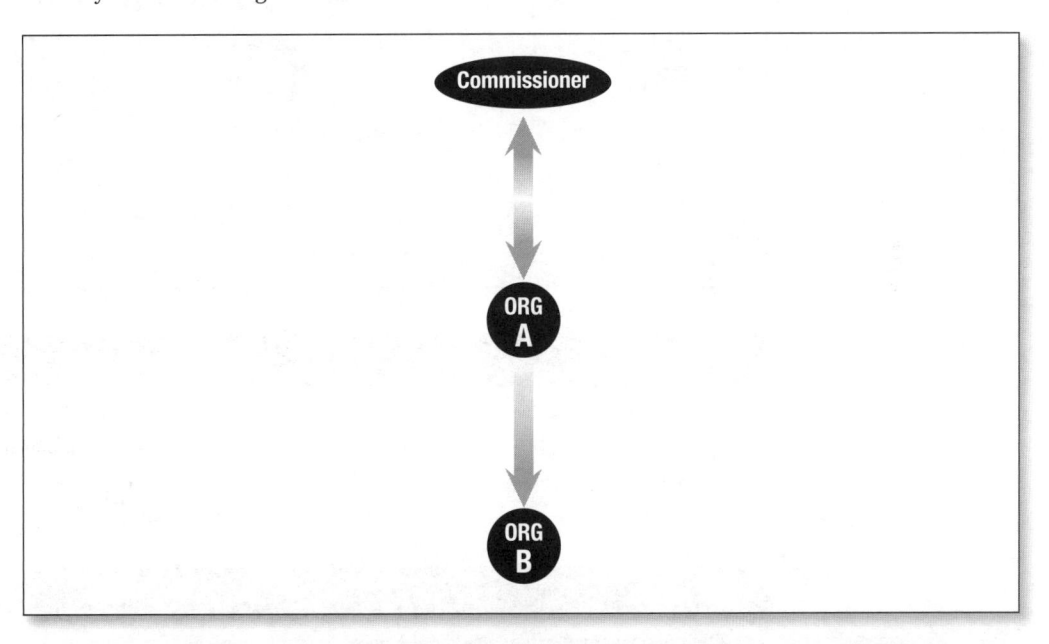

```
        Commissioner
             ↕
           ORG
            A
             ↕
           ORG
            B
```

Potential advantages	Potential disadvantages
■ Can be a way of bringing in smaller or specialist agencies	■ Lines of accountability can get confused
Issues to address	**Business questions**
■ Is there a danger of one organisation dumping difficult or hard work onto another? ■ Can be expensive as both agencies have to take out their management costs from the contract fee	■ Does the contract with the commissioner allow sub-contracting?

Merging

Independent organisations decide to wind up their own affairs and merge with other organisations to create a new and bigger organisation.

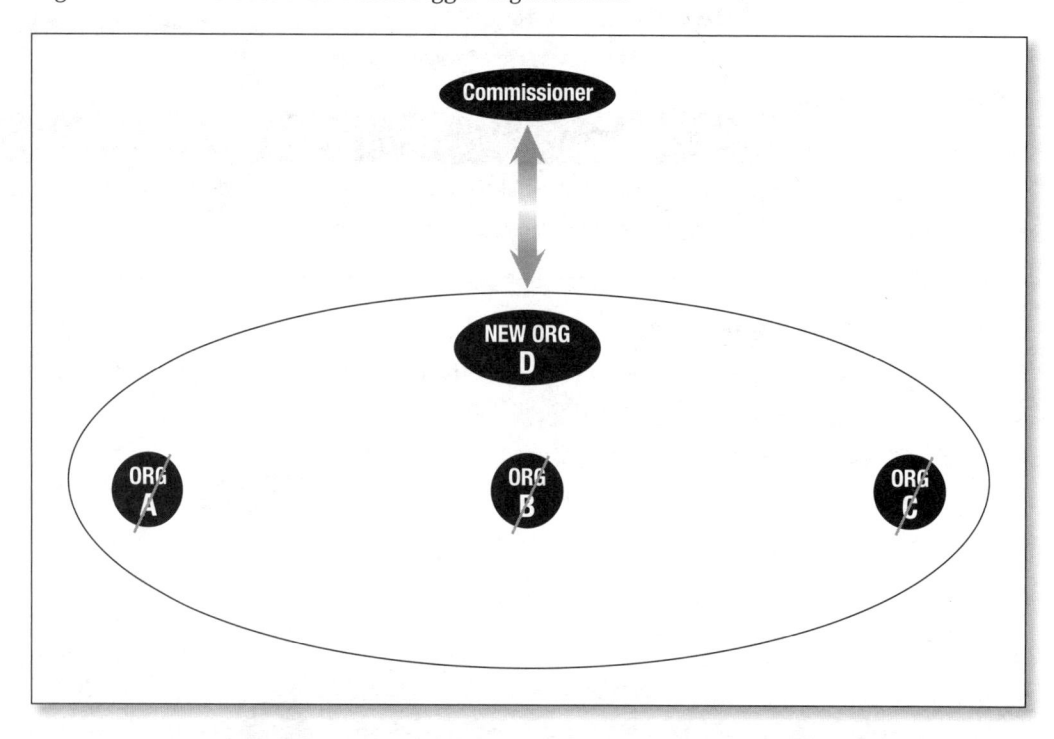

Potential advantages	Potential disadvantages
■ Can be a very clear break with the past ■ A new (and bigger) organisation might be able to win bigger contracts	■ Is there a danger of losing local identity by merging into a bigger organisation? ■ Cost and time involved in the merger process can be significant
Issues to address	**Business questions**
■ Can the new organisation build on the best aspects of the constituent parts?	■ How to ensure continued good will? ■ Tendency for management costs to rise after the merger

Joint working is often hard to achieve. A lack of clear vision, personal egos, strong traditions and an inward-looking culture can often block or work against cooperation between organisations.

Here are three ways in which you can approach the task of joint working.

- **1 Build cooperation gradually**

  Working together in a contract environment can take several different formats. Cooperation can be explored in a gradual and incremental way. A group of healthcare organisations started by meeting together to discuss experience and future plans. This led on to sharing information about future bids and working together to agree a common approach to costing services. Three years on the group is now looking at establishing a consortium to produce joint bids and share out the work amongst the agencies.

- **2 Share strategies**

  A good starting point is to discuss future plans with potential partners. Some organisations have carried out mapping exercises to identify how services fit together and areas for cooperation. This can also lead to individual organisations recognising their strengths.

- **3 Consider the alternatives**
    It is useful to consider the alternative to organisations working together. A manager of a children's' charity commented:

    For us cooperation is not really an option. It is not hard to imagine a situation where all the agencies involved in childcare operate in isolation from each other. Each organisation would scrabble around bidding for whatever contracts were going. There would be duplication and confusion for our users and the opportunity for commissioners to play one off against the other.

Looking ahead to future trends

Although contracts between PSOs and voluntary organisations are not new, there is still a feeling that the process, roles and atmosphere surrounding contracting is still settling down.

We have identified the following trends that could shape the future.

Clearer commissioning

For many parts of the public sector, commissioning is still a new concept. Others are developing approaches to commissioning that focus on identifying current and changing needs, involving users and communities and starting to develop a much more strategic approach. Commissioning needs to be much more than the procuring of services at the lowest price. This movement might mean that commissioning leads to a process where statutory bodies start to question the current approach to service provision and challenge the status quo.

The mechanics of the commissioning process might become more streamlined as systems become established. Having standard contracts and even developments such as e-auctions (where approved providers bid and are appointed on line) might reduce the capacity to negotiate and influence the process.

Knowledge as an asset

Often voluntary organisations play several different roles. As well as delivering services, their contact and involvement with users and communities gives them valuable insight into user needs and expectations. Often voluntary organisations contribute significantly to policy formation, partnership working and service planning. For some organisations the work involved in this role can be considerable – yet it is frequently unrecognised and rarely paid for.

User involvement

Service users or communities are often absent from the commissioning process. Mechanisms to involve users are patchy and lacking. In several areas there is a growing commitment to find ways of actively involving users and communities in making decisions about commissioning priorities, giving feedback about services and increasing the level of choice available.

Some voluntary organisations may find that supporting and facilitating this process becomes a major business for them. Others may find an increasing tension and conflict in being a service provider and simultaneously claiming to 'represent' users to policymakers.

Managing the market

Commissioners play a key role in shaping the market. This can be done in a deliberate way or in more subtle ways. Commissioners can influence the market:

- by how they package services – for example the decision to pull a number of services together into one contract specification might mean that smaller agencies do not feel able to bid
- by their strategy – through determining priorities and highlighting areas for expansion or contraction commissioners can shape the market
- through capacity building – programmes to build the organisational and managerial competence of new or underdeveloped organisations might bring new players (and possibly competition) into the market.

Level playing field

In several areas there are reports of a perceived unfairness in how different organisations are treated. Some voluntary organisations have reported purchasing exercises where they have been subjected to more scrutiny than other agencies. Equally, some private or independent organisations have claimed that voluntary sector providers often get special treatment and support for contracting. As commissioning becomes more established and the legal demands outlined in Chapter 3 become better understood, commissioners will have to demonstrate transparency and equality.

Joint commissioning

There is likely to be a continued push to encourage or require PSOs to work together and overcome traditional demarcation boundaries. Several initiatives are being developed to develop joint or shared commissioning. Greater cooperation between local authorities and primary care trusts and the establishment of joint commissioning teams or groups could mean that voluntary organisations will have to move out of their traditional boundaries and work in a broader field.

New hybrid organisations

There are reports of new forms of organisations entering the market. For example, in a number of areas NHS primary care trusts are in the process of creating social enterprises that will take on direct delivery functions.

Service transfers

As some public bodies start to take on a more commissioning and strategic role there is a possibility that they will start to move away from direct provision. This could lead to asset transfers, for instance where a public sector body transfers an asset (e.g. a playground or a day centre) to an independent provider to operate or where the management of services is contracted out.

CASE STUDY

How will things develop from here... ?

'We are still trying to work out what exactly commissioning means for this department. The commissioning team is made up people with very different backgrounds and skills.

'Some are from a purchasing and procurement background. Their knowledge of the client group and practice is often lacking. They are diligent at making sure that specifications and contracts are watertight. They are very concerned to ensure that things are done properly and legally. They are inclined to be somewhat inflexible and risk averse.

'On the other side are people who come from a service background. They are practitioners who understand the client group, but often struggle with the technicalities of contracting. They are interested in models of service, quality and client feedback. They would prefer to see commissioning as building partnership and collaboration.

'It will be interesting to see how things develop... '

Head of commissioning,
local authority

Further reading and resources

Publications

Compact – Getting it right together, Home Office, 1998

Hearts and Minds: Commissioning from the voluntary sector, Audit Commission, 2007

Improving financial relationships with the third sector: Guidance to funders and purchasers, HM Treasury, 2006

Introductory Pack on Funding and Finance – Guide to procurement and contracting, Institute of Public Finance for the Finance Hub, 2006

Lawrie, Alan, *The Complete Guide to Business and Strategic Planning for Voluntary Organisations*, Directory of Social Change 2007

Partnership in Public Services – An action plan for third sector involvement, Office of the Third Sector, Cabinet Office, 2006

Stand and Deliver: The future for charities providing public service, Charity Commission, 2007

Watt, Brian, *Win Win Negotiation Strategy and Tactics for Third Sector Leaders*, acevo, 2007

Useful websites

Business Link
www.businesslink.gov.uk

Public Law Project
www.publiclawproject.org.uk

Office of Government Commerce
www.ogc.gov.uk

NCVO's Sustainable Funding Project
www.ncvo-vol.org.uk/sfp

Fit 4 Funding (The Charities Information Bureau)
www.fit4funding.org.uk

The Finance Hub
www.financehub.org.uk

Index

A

abuse 55
access 55
accountability 21, 74, 80, 93, 95
ACEVO 40–42
achievability 27, 29, 31
activity 71
advertising 18, 21, 27, 45
advice 59, 64, 71, 76
agreements 2, 5, 9, 10, 12, 19, 53–68, 70
  block 15, 42
  framework 6, 13
  model 54, 56, 57, 64–8
  service level 9, 10, 14, 15, 20, 54, 64
alliance, of providers 94
alternatives 18, 58–9 *passim*, 89, 92, 97
approval, by trustees 56
assertiveness 80
asset transfers 12, 98
assignment 53, 67
assumptions 30, 32, 43, 74, 80, 90
Audit Commission 4, 11, 90

B

bankruptcy 55
benchmarking 47
best value 12, 18–19
bidding 1, 3, 4, 8, 9, 10, 27, 28, 35–52, 85, 86
  two envelope 14, 91
bids 12, 28, 35–52, 86
  joint 92–93
  timetable 18
  writing 5, 35, 45–6, 80, 86
boundaries 70, 85, 98
breach, of contract 2, 25, 56, 66, 67
break clause 77
break points 74, 87
  -even 42
bribery 55
briefing meetings 32
budgets 31, 39
business model 5, 79–84, 87
  grant-led 81
  mixed 82, 83
  project-focused 81–2
business plan 49, 50, 52, 87–9

C

capacity 4, 7, 10, 22, 27, 33, 34, 47, 48, 50, 79, 86–9, 98
case studies 3, 8, 25, 33, 40, 49, 51, 52, 70, 75, 83, 87, 98
cash-flow costs 42
charges 61, 82
Charities Evaluation Services 36
Charity Commission 41
Citizens Advice 36
clients 2, 6, 15, 53, 58, 71 *see also* users
closure 43, 78
  costs 43
codes of good practice 26, 84
collaboration 7, 21, 69, 76
commissioning 3, 4, 10–12, 19–21 *passim*, 76, 77, 89, 90, 97, 98
  framework 20
  influencing 11–12, 20–21
  intelligent 11
  joint 98
  principles 9, 10, 11
communicating 76
community interest company 12
compacts 20, 25, 26
  National 12, 20, 26, 84
compensation 67
competition 3, 6, 9, 17, 18, 21, 37, 54, 89–91
complacency 51
complaints 75, 84, 85
  procedure 55, 61, 75
compliance clauses 55–6
Comprehensive Spending Review 4
confidentiality 55, 61, 62, 67
consideration 10, 12
consortia 10, 93, 96
consultation 3, 7, 10, 12, 18, 20, 24, 25, 26, 31, 34
contacts 77
content, of contract 53–68
cooperation 3, 5, 7, 32, 69, 76, 89, 92–7 *passim*
cost/costing 4, 5, 8, 29, 32, 34, 35, 36, 37, 39–44, 50, 51, 67, 73, 74, 80, 83, 85, 86, 87, 91, 93, 94, 95, 96
  direct 40–42
  fixed 42
  indirect 40, 41, 42, 49, 50
cost recovery, full 6, 13, 26, 40–42
credibility 21, 32, 39
culture 3, 5–6, 37, 39, 54, 70, 79–80

101

Index

D

data protection 55, 62
definitions 12–13, 53, 64, 72
delivery, service 1–4, 38, 47, 48, 50, 71–2, 75, 80, 84, 86
demand 1, 3, 32, 74, 78, 85, 89
dialogue, competitive 21
direct approach 27, 45
dismissal 55
dispute resolution 53, 56, 63, 67, 74–6
donations 6, 7
donors 1, 82
duplication 92, 95, 97
duration, of agreement 53, 60, 65, 66

E

early warning system 74
E-auction 13, 97
email alerts/lists 22, 23, 45
employment tribunal 55
equal treatment 18, 22, 98
equality of opportunity 26, 55, 62
European Journal 12, 13, 17
European Union 9, 17, 18, 25
   Court of Justice 18
   Procurement Directives 17, 20, 25
evaluation 13, 36, 50, 53, 86
   of outcomes 3, 5, 37, 53–4, 61
   of specification 28–34
   of tenders 12, 19, 22, 23–4, 35, 46, 91
evidence 2, 8, 11–12, 37, 38, 46, 48, 49, 50, 52, 86
evolution 83–4
exit strategy 77–8
expectations 1, 2, 6, 11, 27, 31, 32, 44, 46–7, 51, 70, 73, 74, 79, 97
experience 11, 37, 38, 45–6, 48, 50, 51, 91

F

failure 30, 55, 56
feedback, user 10, 12, 19, 20, 23, 38, 74, 76, 77, 86, 97
fees 6, 42–3, 44, 53, 82
fit, organisational 33, 46, 48, 56, 80, 87
fixed-term contract 77–8, 82
follow up 57
force majeure 67
funding 2, 6, 7, 9, 54, 69, 80–81
   block 6

G

gaps 11, 30, 39, 45
goodwill costs 43

grants 1–3 *passim*, 6, 9, 26, 79, 81
   aid 1–2, 9, 42–3, 79, 81, 82 *see also* relationships
growth, organisational 88, 92

H

health and safety 55, 62
help, asking for 59
hidden agendas 30, 59
hybrid organisations 98

I

identity 5, 96
illegality 68
impact 13, 71–2
implications, organisational 79–88
income 39, 80, 87
   sources 5, 82, 83, 84, 87
indemnity 53
independence 1, 2, 5, 6, 79, 82, 84, 86, 89, 94
indicators, performance 4, 12, 36
inflation 54
information 5, 17, 24, 26, 39, 52, 54, 55, 58, 61, 62, 65, 71, 76, 87, 94, 96
infrastructure 37, 41, 42, 82, 84, 87, 91
initiative, taking 6, 76
inputs 13, 71
insurance 3, 46, 53, 62, 65
interviews 35, 47–8
   selection 22
investment 5, 7, 12, 21, 77
Investors in People 36
invitations to tender 13, 19, 22–3, 26, 52
involvement 4, 10, 11–12, 59
   of trustees 85
   of users 10, 31, 50, 67, 80, 84, 90, 97
ISO 9000 36

J

joint service plan 94
joint ventures 93–4
Jordans Charities Administration Service 64
'journey travelled' 73
judicial review 24–5

K

knowledge 38–9, 97

L

language 1, 4, 12–14, 46, 49, 53, 56, 64
law/legal issues 1, 2 5, 10, 17, 24–6 *passim*, 33, 56, 62, 68, 85, 86, 91

lead body 92–93
Leather, Dame Suzi 41
liability 56
  limitation of 53, 65, 66
list, approved 12, 22, 45
lobbying 6, 30, 94
local authorities 1, 3, 6, 9, 12, 17, 18, 20, 24, 26, 31, 45, 54, 70, 77, 91, 98
Local Government White Paper (2006) 3
'loss leader' 44, 91

M

management 1, 5, 10, 80, 82, 84, 85, 87, 92
  contract 4–5, 15, 69–70, 74, 76
  costs 42
managing contracts 1, 4–5, 10, 19, 60, 69–78, 79–80, 87
  prerequisites 4–5
mapping exercises 96
marketing 37, 45, 86
markets 11, 44, 89–91, 98
  domination 89, 90
  provider-led 89
measuring 13, 71–76 *passim*, 80, 86
  over- 71
merging 96
milestones 13
MIND 36
misrepresentation 56
mission 80, 85
monitoring 2, 9, 13, 39, 53, 54, 62, 69, 70, 71, 73–4, 80
monopoly 21

N

needs, user 3, 4, 10–11 *passim*, 19, 21, 31, 32, 46, 48, 50, 74, 78, 90, 95, 97
negotiating 1, 19, 21, 24, 54, 55, 56, 57–9, 86
  unblocking 59
networks 12, 36, 39
neutrality, competitive 11
New Philanthropy Capital 40–41
NHS 2, 9, 17, 83, 84
niche services 2, 7, 90
non-compliance 23, 25, 53, 55, 75
notice 12, 17, 55, 63, 65, 66, 67

O

obligations 2, 24, 65
Office of Third Sector 10
opportunities, identifying/analysing 5, 27–34
  responding to 27

outcome-based contract 15
outcomes 2, 6, 10, 12, 13, 21, 27–9, 31, 46, 48, 50, 61, 71–3, 77, 80, 86
output 2, 9, 13, 40, 71–3, 80, 84, 86
outsourcing 19, 95
overdraft charges 42

P

pace-setting 85–6
packaging services 98
participation 12
partnerships 3, 5, 7, 12, 13, 21, 26, 69, 97, 98
  public-private 20
payment 15, 53, 54, 60, 65, 90
performance measurement 13, 69, 71–4 *passim*, 76, 80, 86
permanent contract 77
planning 5, 10, 21, 34, 57, 73, 76, 79, 85, 87–9, 92, 94–5, 97, 99
players, in market 90
PQASSO 36
presentations 35, 47–52 *passim*
price/pricing 11, 13, 14, 35, 36, 37, 39, 44, 50, 53, 54, 60, 64, 65, 74, 91
primary care trusts 17, 20, 31, 33, 52, 83, 98
priorities 10, 21, 76, 87, 97, 98
private sector 3, 4, 9, 11, 90
proactive approach 1, 45
problems 54–5, 70, 71, 74–6, 77, 85, 89–90
procurement 9, 11, 13, 14, 17–26 *passim*
  EU rules 17
  principles 18
  procedures 19, 21, 21–3
  Regulations 17, 19, 25–6
projects 28, 71, 81–2
  contract 6, 16
proportionality 18
public authorities 1, 2, 21, 22, 24, 79
public service contracts 6, 17, 18
public service organisations 3, 7, 9–11, 14–15, 17–20, 22–4 *passim*, 45, 70, 76, 97, 98
purchasers/purchasing 35–6, 42–3, 44, 53, 54, 55, 89, 90, 98
purpose, of agreement 53, 60

Q

qualifications 18, 91
quality 14, 35–6, 37, 50, 53, 63, 89, 91
  assurance 14, 36, 50, 61
questionnaire 22–3
  pre-qualification 13, 19, 22
questions 59
  so what? 47
  what if? 32, 54, 74, 85

R

recognition, mutual 18, 84
recording/records 11, 38, 54, 55, 59, 61, 65
Regulations 17, 19, 25, 26
relationships 1–7, 31, 80
  contractual 1–4 *passim*, 21, 69–70, 74, 76–7, 80, 87
  funder–supplicant 69
  grant-aid 1–2, 3, 54, 69, 79
  master–sub-contractor 69
relevance 33
reliability 35–6, 37, 50, 91
renewal, of contract 77
repeat/additional works 23
reporting 70, 73, 76
reputation 32, 56, 58, 70, 78
retendering 56
review meetings 41, 62, 64, 73
rights 5, 23
  access 55
  intellectual property 23, 64, 66
risk 4, 5, 6, 10, 14, 27, 31, 32–4, 50, 70, 74, 80, 83–5 *passim*, 88, 93
rolling contract 77

S

sample contract 60–63
savings, efficiency 54
saying no 5, 33
scope of service 27
service contract 6, 17, 18 *see also* agreements
shocks 77
signals 59
skills 5, 6, 31, 33, 34, 38, 50, 51, 78, 79, 83, 86, 88
social enterprises 12, 14, 98
specialisation 95
specification 4, 12, 13, 14, 18, 19, 22, 23, 27–34, 35–7, 44, 47, 51–2, 53, 55, 57, 60, 62, 64, 68, 89, 98
spot/unit purchase contract 15
squeezing out 24
staff 32, 43–4, 55, 56, 61, 62, 78, 79
  transferring *see* TUPE
standards 18, 36, 50, 53, 64, 65, 68, 86, 89, 91
standstill period/clause 23
start-up 81
  costs 43, 82
strategy 3, 4, 5, 11, 33, 34, 41, 45, 46, 76, 77–8, 80, 87, 88, 96–8
strengths 37, 38, 80
sub-contracting 10, 14, 53, 62, 67, 69, 95
subsidisation 41, 42, 44, 82
  cross- 83
success 77
supplies contract 18

supply 89
support 5, 40, 42, 82, 84, 87
  costs 40, 86
  in-kind 81
sustainability 32, 79–83

T

targets 3, 11, 21, 28, 29, 30, 90
taxation 2, 43 *see also* VAT
tendering 9, 13, 14, 19, 20, 22–4, 26, 52, 56
  invitations to 13, 19, 22–3, 27, 52
  questionnaire 22–3
  timetable 19, 22
  two envelope 14, 91
termination, of contract 52, 55, 63, 66, 75–8
time-based contract 15
track record 36, 37, 48, 50, 51, 80, 91
training 20, 36, 37, 76
transaction costs 86
transparency 10, 18, 24, 98
Treasury 39
trends 11, 73, 83, 97–8
trustees 1, 5, 33, 50, 56, 58, 59, 79, 84, 85–6
TUPE 14, 43–4, 51, 56
  costs of 43–4
types, of contract 15, 18

U

underspending 31, 54
unenforceability 68
unincorporated charity 56
unique selling proposition 37, 90
urgency 23
users 3–5 *passim*, 30, 31, 34, 46, 48, 50, 55, 61, 62, 72, 74, 75–6, 78, 80, 90, 97

V

value added 4, 6, 12, 21, 38–9, 42, 46, 50, 74, 87, 91, 92
value for money 7, 9, 14, 17, 18, 19, 23, 42
values 5, 6, 27, 33, 35, 80, 85
variations, in contract 53, 54, 63, 67, 73
VAT 2, 43, 51, 53, 56, 60, 65
vision 85, 89
voluntary sector 3, 4, 9, 11, 19, 18, 26, 42, 54
volunteers 39, 55, 61, 62, 79

W

waivers 68
walk away point 58, 59
weaknesses 37
working together 3, 6, 7, 89, 92–97 *see also* cooperation